GEOFFREY MADAN'S
NOTEBOOKS

GEOFFREY MADAN'S NOTEBOOKS

A SELECTION

Edited by
J. A. GERE AND JOHN SPARROW

With a Foreword by
THE RT. HON. HAROLD MACMILLAN, O.M.

Oxford   New York
OXFORD UNIVERSITY PRESS

Oxford University Press, Walton Street, Oxford OX2 6DP

London New York Toronto
Delhi Bombay Calcutta Madras Karachi
Kuala Lumpur Singapore Hong Kong Tokyo
Nairobi Dar es Salaam Cape Town
Melbourne Auckland

and associated companies in
Beirut Berlin Ibadan Mexico City Nicosia

Oxford is a trade mark of Oxford University Press

First published 1981 by Oxford University Press
First issued as an Oxford University Press paperback 1984
Reprinted 1985

British Library Cataloguing in Publication Data

Madan, Geoffrey
Geoffrey Madan's notebooks.
1. Quotations, English
I. Title. II. Gere, J. A.
III. Sparrow, John
080   PN6081

ISBN 0–19–281870–8

Library of Congress Cataloging in Publication Data

Madan, Geoffrey, 1895–1947.
Geoffrey Madan's Notebooks.
(Oxford paperbacks)
1. Commonplace-books. I. Gere, John A. II. Sparrow,
John Hanbury Angus, 1906–   . III. Title. IV. Title:
Notebooks.
[PN6245.M27 1984]   082   84–10090
ISBN 0–19–281870–8 (pbk.)

Printed in Great Britain by
Richard Clay (The Chaucer Press) Ltd
Bungay, Suffolk

CONTENTS

Foreword by the Rt. Hon. Harold Macmillan, o.m.   vii

Introduction   xi

    I. BEAUTY, POINT, AND CHARM   1

   II. HUMOROUS AND MEMORABLE   9

  III. ACADEMICA   21

  IV. APHORISMS AND REFLECTIONS   27

   V. PHRASES AND DESCRIPTIONS   37

  VI. EXTRACTS AND SUMMARIES   41

 VII. VINIANA   83

VIII. DE PECUNIA   87

  IX. ANECDOTES   89

   X. RECOLLECTIONS AND THINGS SEEN   97

  XI. LIVRES SANS NOM   103

FOREWORD

THOSE of us who have reached extreme old age become gradually reconciled to increasing infirmities, mental and physical. The body develops, with each passing year, fresh weaknesses. Our legs no longer carry us; eyesight begins to fail, and hearing becomes feebler. Even with the mind, the process of thought seems largely to decrease in its power and intensity; and if we are wise we come to accept these frailties and develop, like all invalids, our own particular skills in avoiding or minimizing them. But there is one aspect of the mind which seems to operate in a peculiar fashion. While memory becomes gradually weaker in respect of recent happenings and even of the leading events of middle age, yet it appears to become increasingly strong as regards the years of childhood and youth. It is as if the new entries played into an ageing computer become gradually less effective while the original stores remain as strong as ever.

This phenomenon has the result that as the memory of so many much more important matters begins to fade, those of many years ago become sharper than before. The recent writings on the tablets of the mind grow quickly weak as if made by a light brush or soft pencil. Those of the earliest years become more and more deeply etched. The pictures which they recall are as fresh as ever. Indeed they seem to strengthen with each passing year.

When, therefore, I received the invitation of the editors of this volume of *Geoffrey Madan's Notebooks* my hesitation was due not to any haziness in my recollections of this quite exceptional man, but rather to my doubts as to whether I could find the words to recall his picture to those who knew him well or to give some impression of him to those to whom he is only a vague memory.

Although I had known Geoffrey from Eton years (he was one Election below me in College) it was really at Oxford in those halcyon years immediately before the first War that I learned something of his character and talents. In appearance he was strikingly handsome, with something of the look of those young men who stand about to no apparent purpose in many Renaissance paintings. He conveyed with all his physical beauty a certain air of detachment which enhanced its charm. The quiet, almost immobile, way in which he comported himself in conversation added to this illusion. He had many friends at Oxford in all circles. He by no means confined his company to those who could fully appreciate his intellectual gifts and his extraordinarily comprehensive mind. He had many, and some unexpected, friends. He liked then, as he did throughout his life, good food, good wine, and an atmosphere of quiet conversation, often witty, often learned, and never dull.

At Oxford he and I were both intimate friends of Ronald Knox, then Anglican Chaplain at Trinity College, and it was in his circle that Geoffrey shone. He was good company and seemed always happy, and he enjoyed social contacts. Yet there was something rather mysterious behind this young face which set him apart. At first I was rather shy of him, for he was the kind of man before whom one would fear to say something foolish or banal or commit an intellectual solecism. Yet this was only an instinct reflecting my appreciation of the extraordinary refinement and delicacy of his mind. While he had nothing at all of pedantry or prudery, yet he clearly shrank from what might suggest the brutal or the coarse. He had no fear, as he was to prove afterwards when the War came, but he had a natural dislike of ugliness and dirt and therefore in due course was to suffer severely. The years of war parted us and it was only at the beginning of the twenties that I began to see him again. Like so many of the friends of youth, as opposed to the acquaintances of later years, one could feel able with him to take up an unfinished conversation begun several years before exactly at the point where it had been left off. These are indeed the true friendships of special value. However old these friends become they see themselves and feel themselves still as young. Nor do these relations have to be maintained by continual nurture. They are so deeply rooted that they flourish so long as life lasts.

In the following years I saw Geoffrey only from time to time. In London he made a large acquaintance, especially among authors and artists, as well as with all those who appreciated the delicacy of his wit and the remarkable range of his reading. He was a true scholar without any of the affectations of scholarship, and, as these *Notebooks* show, he had a peculiar sense of humour which could find something to tickle the fancy even in the most dull and boring passage in a parliamentary speech or an editorial pronouncement.

Of Greek and Latin his knowledge was profound and extensive and equal, I would say, to that of Ronald Knox himself. In French he was widely read. But it was his use of epigrammatic English that made his conversation memorable. Yet it was never strained. It seemed often that he would prefer to listen rather than intervene with the eagerness of so many keen conversationalists. This suited not only his slightly sceptical temperament but also his exquisite good manners.

In every age there have been men whose memory will always be recorded for outstanding achievements in war, in art, in politics, or in literature. There will be other figures – more shadowy, more difficult to reconstruct, and yet as important in their contribution to the social and intellectual life of their time. Those who have not known them, or heard them speak, find it difficult to realize why the memory of such figures is cherished by their contemporaries.

This volume will serve two purposes. It will be cherished by his surviving friends and recall vividly to their memories Geoffrey Madan's unique personality. To others these *Notebooks* will give pleasure from their intrinsic value and also reveal a clue to the special affection felt for him by a devoted circle of friends.

HAROLD MACMILLAN

October 1980

INTRODUCTION

WHEN Geoffrey Madan came up from Eton to Balliol in 1913, at the age of eighteen, he seemed to be on the threshold of a brilliant career. Like his friend and older contemporary Ronald Knox, also an Eton Colleger and Balliol Scholar, he was the fine flower of that rarefied and uniquely English literary culture, based on intensive study of the Classics, which Eton offers to the few who are able to profit from it. But, as things turned out, the formal successes of his life had all been achieved by the time he left school.

Geoffrey Spencer Madan was born in Oxford on 6 February 1895. His father, Falconer Madan, was a Fellow of Brasenose and Bodley's Librarian; like Disraeli, Geoffrey could have boasted that he was 'born in a library'. From Summer Fields he won the top scholarship at Eton in 1907. During his first year the Master in College was Cyril Alington, who was succeeded by Aymer Whitworth. A natural classic, he carried off many prizes, especially for composition: Latin Prose, Latin Verse, Greek Iambics, Latin Essay. As his widow Marjorie Madan wrote, 'Greek was the familiar medium in which he excelled'; but he also won an English verse prize, edited the *Eton College Chronicle*, and presided over the Essay Society. He won the School Chess Tournament at the age of fourteen, but evidently decided to waste no more time on that. In 1912 he was awarded a classical scholarship at Balliol and in his last year he was elected to Pop.

This brief account of his school career suggests a conventional paragon, a prize-pupil; but Geoffrey Madan was very much more than that. The originality of his mind and the quality of his scholarship showed themselves in a description of Eton in Herodotean Greek, a *tour de force* which achieved the rare distinction of being 'sent up for play', thus gaining the School a whole holiday. A. B. Ramsay, one of the masters who taught him, described *Herodotus at Eton** as a work 'of great erudition and humour', adding

---

* Printed at Eton 1912, its dedication: 'C.A.A [lington], *Ludicras has primitias Dedico*'. In the previous year also he had been 'sent up for play', for his Greek Iambics.

that Madan's devotion to the byways of scholarship probably prevented him from achieving all he might have done in the way of more conventional academic success. But Ramsay went on to admit that he was a first-rate classic of the linguistic school.

His affection for Eton itself, its *genius loci* and its personalities, was passionate and lifelong. William Cory; Francis Warre Cornish, the Vice-Provost, and his even more notable wife; H. E. Luxmoore; Henry Broadbent; A. C. Ainger; C. M. Wells; George Lyttelton – these and many other Eton names occur often in his Notebooks. The young Geoffrey sagely knew how to exploit the rich seams of learning, discrimination, and reminiscence embedded in the minds of his elders; his precocious sensitivity and tact enabled him to touch their hearts without chilling or bruising them. 'He had the rare gift (rare in youth)', wrote Percy Lubbock, 'of approaching his elders with all the advantages of his youth, and those so many, without spoiling or wasting them (after the manner of clever youth in general) by shyness in any of its protean forms.'

Mrs. Cornish had received him, when a nervous new arrival, 'as though [he] had been an ambassador', and his Notebooks contain a tantalizingly brief allusion to a conversation with her: 'Mrs. Cornish to me on Bywater before we went into lunch, 1908.' Marjorie Madan charmingly defended the inclusion of this scrap in her privately issued selection from the Notebooks:

What did Mrs Cornish say about Ingram Bywater, the scholar with the romantic name and the fine bookplate, in whom G. M. at the age of 13 was already interested? Not a flashing, single sentence, but part of a conversation; there is now no echo of the words, and yet one is reluctant to let the little scene disappear unrecorded. How delightfully memorable Mrs Cornish must have been before going into lunch with that young responsive guest. . . .

By urging Geoffrey to send his Herodotean pastiche to Arthur Benson, formerly a successful Eton housemaster and now, at the age of fifty, a Fellow of Magdalene College, Cambridge, Mrs. Cornish initiated a friendship and a correspondence which continued uninterruptedly until Benson's death in 1925. Benson was immediately *épris* with this 'tall, handsome, well-dressed, rather self-conscious boy, with a slight outward cast of eye . . . a beautiful fellow to look at . . . ingenuous, simple, clever: he has that sort of youthful shyness which is not diffidence so much as deference'. Percy

Lubbock also left a description of Geoffrey as he was then: 'He seemed to be ringed round with fresh and transparent air, not over-mild, in which nothing graceless or formless or nerveless could live – but which brightened all else.'

At Michaelmas 1913 Geoffrey Madan went up to Balliol and began reading for Classical Moderations with Cyril Bailey as his tutor. He continued to pursue out-of-the-way studies as well as the regular curriculum; for example, he developed an interest in Byzantine Greek into which he attempted a verse rendering of St. Luke's Gospel. He joined the Union and, in Balliol, the Arnold and Brackenbury Societies and he was elected to the exclusive Annandale; he made lifelong friends, among them Harold Macmillan, Cyril Asquith (whose father was then Prime Minister), and Ronald Knox, still at that time an Anglican and Chaplain and Fellow of Trinity. In the vacations he stayed with Arthur Benson in Cambridge, on holiday in Worcestershire, and at the Bensons' family home in Sussex.

Geoffrey was one of a succession of young men whom Benson – with complete propriety, needless to say – permitted himself the indulgence of adoring. His particular attraction lay not only in his good looks but also in his command of the subtleties of linguistic scholarship, his intellectual sophistication, and – of all bonds one of the strongest – a congenial sense of humour. Percy Lubbock speaks of his 'love of paradox – his rich exaggerations and the virtuosity of his phrase. (He and A.C.B. were particularly matched there – they fired each other.)' Geoffrey's appreciation of the individual quality of the older man's wit is evident in his two pen-portraits, 'A Later Friendship' and 'Arthur Benson's Notebooks', published respectively in 1925 and 1927 (see p. xviii). Benson, for his part, recalled quoting two lines of Tennyson which Geoffrey, 'with only a moment's thought', rendered into Greek hexameters; after a day spent with him on Bredon Hill he wrote in his diary:

Let me say frankly that I doubt if I have ever in my life felt so much in love with a human being as I felt today, nor come so near to one who seemed to me to realize more closely what I mean by beauty, grace and charm.

Geoffrey had hardly begun to make friends in a wider world than those of Eton and Oxford and Cambridge, when the entire world was overwhelmed by the disaster that was to cut short innumerable lives and friendships. Through Cyril Asquith he soon came to know other members of the family; in the Long Vacation of 1914 he stayed with the Bernard Berensons at Settignano before joining a reading-party at F. F. Urquhart's ('Sligger's') châlet at Chamonix. At the beginning of August he returned to England after a difficult journey across a Continent already at war, and immediately volunteered for the Army. After dinner one night, in the prevailing atmosphere of frantic and short-lived euphoria, he and Cys Asquith succeeded in downing twelve glasses each in a Benedictine-drinking contest. Geoffrey was commissioned in the King's Own Royal Lancaster Regiment and just before Christmas, after a farewell dinner with Benson at the Royal Bath Hotel in Southampton, he embarked for the Front.

Captain Madan came back from the War in November 1918, after serving at Gallipoli and in Salonika, France, Italy, and Mesopotamia. In that last campaign, early in 1916, he was wounded; his wounds were not serious, but, in the words of his friend John Murray (later Principal of the University College of the South-West at Exeter), 'Mesopotamia shook him, and shook him for life, more perhaps than friends mostly realized.' Letters from Benson (they wrote to each other once a week), visits to him on leave, and the remembered vision of Eton, all sustained his spirits. 'The elms of Eton,' Marjorie Madan later wrote, 'and the sunlight and shadows of that temperate valley, are recalled constantly and with longing in Geoffrey's letters from Gallipoli, Mesopotamia, an Indian hospital.'

But no schoolboy could survive the War: Geoffrey came back a young man, scarred but hardened. He returned to Balliol for the Trinity Term of 1919, but came down without taking his degree. Later that same year he married Marjorie, the elder daughter of Sir Saxton Noble, to whom, one day, on her lawn at Eton, Mrs. Cornish, 'that splendid creator of occasions', had introduced him. In 1920 he went into the City, but after an attack of meningitis in 1924, which left his health permanently impaired, he thankfully retired from an occupation that he found increasingly uncongenial. The enjoyment of a private income enabled him to cultivate his leisure: 'If never rich,' Marjorie Madan wrote, 'he was freed from anxiety in an atmosphere of security, French cooking and gaiety.' They had one child, Nicola, born in 1920.

The Madans' circumstances were never luxurious, but they were able to live a comfortable and discriminating life in London.

Geoffrey became a connoisseur of wine and developed an expert knowledge of old silver, of which he made a small but choice collection. Books, however, remained his greatest interest: 'a profound and passionate bibliophile,' wrote Cyril Asquith, 'he tasted tomes and libraries as epicures sample wines. Conversely he drank wine with a bookish palate, specializing in those great clarets which are "for advanced students only".' The bookplate reserved for his more precious books bore a legend, '*Ex libris nobilioribus apud G.M. hospitantibus*', inspired by the title '*Elenchus librorum vetustiorum apud . . . hospitantium*' devised by Ingram Bywater for the catalogue of his great collection of *incunabula*. The outstanding feature of Geoffrey's less magnificent but no less fastidiously chosen library was a collection relating to Horace Walpole and to Dr. Johnson and his circle, a bibliographic field in which he became something of a specialist. His most prized acquisition – his wife went so far as to describe it as 'a romance of his life' – was a holograph manuscript of Swinburne's *Ave atque Vale* which appeared in a country sale, only to be snapped up by a rival collector. He eventually secured it by selling other books, and his widow gave it in his memory to Eton.

But books for Geoffrey were not mere collector's items: as the pages that follow show, his reading was extraordinarily wide and he had a keen appreciation of the striking sentence and the significant anecdote. As a matter of course he kept up his interest in the Classics, but he also read widely in English and French memoirs, collections of aphorisms, biographies, essays, fiction, history, poetry, newspapers (with particular attention to obituaries and Law Reports), periodicals ranging from school magazines to the *New Statesman* and *The Economist*, and even Parliamentary Reports.

He also explored minor byways of literature such as the Sherlock Holmes saga. Cyril Asquith, whom during the Second World War he regularly met at Brooks's for half an hour or so in the evening, recalled their game of gazing down into St. James's Street from a window of the club and attempting to apply Holmes's methods to the classification of the passers-by:

Someone paused on the pavement with his back to us. G.M. (who, I noticed, cast himself as a rule in the part of Mycroft, the 'profounder' of the two observers): 'Can you, Sherlock, deduce nothing from that nuque?' C.A.: 'An average-adjuster, plainly.' G.M.: 'I am distressed, Sherlock. Is it possible that you cannot distinguish an average-adjuster from an actuary, by the set of his cravat?' Honours were even in this case, as the stranger then turned, revealing the cravatless throat – he wore an ordinary tie – and the distinguished profile of Sir Edward Marsh. (Indeed, I remember no case in which our conjectures were verified.)

Already in 1923 Arthur Benson found Geoffrey surprisingly well-informed about the private lives of famous people. It would be misleading to imply that he was a recluse, content to view the world from the seclusion of a library. While not a sociable man in any sense of the word, he collected – in addition to silver, wine, and books – London clubs; of these institutions, which he seems to have regarded largely as places of refuge, he was at one time believed to be a member simultaneously of eleven or twelve – though never admitting to more than six or seven. No less important to him than books was the conversation of his friends. These extended over no less wide a range – from churchmen, lawyers, bankers, and politicians to men of letters, connoisseurs, and dons. They included Cyril Asquith, Arnold Bennett, Arthur Benson, Winston and Clementine Churchill, O. T. Falk, Dean Inge, Desmond MacCarthy, H. G. Wells, Mr. and Mrs. Yates Thompson, and G. M. Young. As Shane Leslie recalled, he 'collected good talk and carefully bottled a good story – he loved the subtle, the bewildering, the academical, all that was like a rich distilled liqueur which he retained in infinitesimally small bottles for private use, leaving eventually the massed collections like a cellar to be tasted to his own memory.' That 'cellar' consists of the series of Notebooks in which he would type (very neatly) or inscribe in a bold hand whatever had struck him during the day in the way of anecdotes, phrases, quotations, anagrams, or jokes, many of them jotted down on the spot with what Marjorie Madan vividly described as 'the quick, covert gesture with pencil and paper'.

His own conversation and the elusively oblique humour of his letters more than repaid his friends for all that they had unknowingly contributed to his store of phrase and anecdote. 'There were certain worlds in which we had separately wandered', Shane Leslie continues, 'and could always instantly exchange our notes and anecdotes – a phantasy world stretching between Luxmoore's Eton and Monty James's King's and Arthur Benson's Magdalene. It is a world which has passed away, leaving fragments, fragilities of humour with certain choice spirits, half-sayings, quarter-tones which never reached the paragraph and seldom the sentence – whole commentaries could be written on single lines.' Ronald Knox has also left us a description of his talk: 'How admirably that sudden drop into a lower key, so characteristic of his conversation, brought out the flavour of the saying, the anecdote! He was all of a piece; personality blended with the chaste furniture of his mind to make the complete humanist. . . . No one, at least so I found, had less of the scholar's bluntness, impatience, crotchetiness.'

The aphorism particularly appealed to him and was a literary form that he himself attempted. In a 'causerie' in *The Times* (18 June 1959), 'George Cloyne' (a pseudonym of the critic Alan Pryce-Jones) observed that 'there *are* good modern aphorists. . . . I have not forgotten Geoffrey Madan.' Every Christmas from 1929 to 1933 Geoffrey sent out, as a present for his friends, an elegantly printed booklet, entitled *Livre sans Nom*, containing fifty-two carefully chosen items from his Notebooks. Aphorisms tended to predominate in these selections, and in 1934 his Christmas offering was a smaller booklet containing *Twelve Reflections* of his own composition, under the initials L.S.N. He had already insinuated himself pseudonymously into the *Livres sans Nom*, in French as 'M. Heyguet' (a reference to the Eton master, A. C. G. Heygate) and in English (the fruit of a collaboration with G. M. Young) as 'Henry Ward'. The five *Livres sans Nom*, and a sixth such selection which was never printed, are included at the end of this book, together with *Twelve Reflections*.

It would be wholly misleading to leave the reader with the impression that Geoffrey Madan was an affable, warm-hearted man. After his death, John Murray wrote of his 'uncanny aloofness, as if he had stepped from the everywhere and the nowhere into here; as if, in his curious way, he was in time but not of it'. In consequence of his wartime experiences, to which his severe illness in 1924 was probably in great part due, he suffered from, and showed, what his widow described as an 'undercurrent of stress, which, running beneath a sense of privilege, made it hard for him to accept the terms of ordinary life'. Though always proud of his daughter, he was not fond of children, and he was not an easy father. His mischief could sometimes hurt: he had a particular dislike of dogs, and a schoolfriend of Nicola's, who had rashly brought her mother's Pekingese with her to the Madans' flat, found him preparing a box in which 'to take it to the vet to be put down'. In the words of an obituary notice, intended for *The Times* but never sent: 'A genius for friendship with all and sundry, infectious enthusiasm, selfless devotion to progressive causes, a deep and touching love of animals and of natural beauty – he would not have claimed for himself any of these so frequent attributes of the lately dead.' Cyril Asquith stated roundly that he was 'never at any pains to court popularity, and indeed sometimes seemed anxious to avert it: "X", he wrote, "is a man of unapproachable stupidity; when we meet I invariably tell him so";' but, Asquith went on to say, Geoffrey was 'quite unable not to inspire the strongest affection in people in the most varied walks of life, once they caught his rather elusive "wave length"'.

Geoffrey Madan died suddenly in London on 6 July 1947. His ashes were scattered in Luxmoore's Garden at Eton, a place that had remained, in Marjorie Madan's words, 'part of his life to his last day'.

When Geoffrey Madan was young, in the days before the First World War, it must have seemed that a brilliant career lay before him in virtually any direction he chose. But even if the War had not to some extent thrown him off his balance, the excessively fastidious quality of his mind might have inhibited ambition and stifled accomplishment. As it was, his most lasting achievement – an essentially private one – was the compilation of his Notebooks. Ronald Knox said, 'If he had lived, he might have written an exquisite book of reminiscences or perhaps THE anthology; his gift was for anthologizing, he had an unerring eye for the alpha double plus.' If he had ever contemplated such an anthology – containing perhaps, to use his own phrase, 'the forgotten sayings of great men, and the great sayings of forgotten men' – his Notebooks would have furnished the material for it; while his ability as a writer of reminiscences is demonstrated by a few brilliant pen-portraits, mostly of friends, published in the late 1920s.*

*'Arthur Benson's Notebooks' (*Cornhill Magazine*, Feb. 1927), 'Henry Elford Luxmoore' (ibid., June 1927 and *Etoniana*, no. 121, 30 Nov. 1968), 'William Cory' (*Cornhill Magazine*, Aug. 1928), 'Arthur Hallam: one who "Perish'd in the Green"' (*The Times*, 15 Sept. 1933), 'The Reform of English' (*Saturday Review*, 17 April 1920), 'A Later Friendship' (from *Arthur Christopher Benson as seen by some Friends*, ed. E. H. Ryle, 1925), 'The Rev. the Hon. E. Lyttelton' (*Etoniana, ut supra*), 'The Rev. C. A. Alington', 'A Short View of Mussolini', 'Montagu Norman: omne magnificum pro ignoto' and three Eton juvenilia are printed, with some abridgement of 'Arthur Benson's Notebooks', in *Geoffrey Madan, a Memoir* [by his sister, Beatrice Brocklebank], issued privately in 1984. The first four are also reprinted in Marjorie Madan's selection from the Notebooks, and 'Mussolini' and 'Montagu Norman' on pp. 100 ff. of the present volume in the section headed 'Recollections and Things Seen'.

After his death Marjorie Madan prepared a selection from the Notebooks, and in 1949 sixty copies in duplicated typescript were distributed to relations and friends and to a few libraries (Eton, Balliol, Brooks's Club, The London Library). This selection was accompanied by an admirably vivid introductory note by her and appreciations of Geoffrey by six of his friends: Cyril Asquith, Ronald Knox, Shane Leslie, Percy Lubbock, John Murray, and A. B. Ramsay. The extent to which we have drawn on this material in the present Introduction will be evident to the reader.

By kind permission of Mrs. Madan and her daughter, Lady Campbell of Croy, an entirely fresh selection from the full text of the Notebooks has been made, though much, of course, is common to both selections. Geoffrey Madan's notes, even when he had transcribed them, were no more than *aides-mémoire*. Such explanatory matter as accompanies them is often so laconic as now to be incomprehensible. If he had prepared his notes for publication, he would certainly have expanded the initials used to denote his sources and have added whatever was necessary to bring out the point of the quotation or anecdote. In doing this, so far as we have been able, we have gratefully incorporated editorial explanations and comments from the earlier volume, and others subsequently contributed by its readers. So far as possible, we have also verified and where necessary corrected quotations and an occasional apparent misattribution: like many people with an excellent memory, Madan was unduly inclined to rely on it. The two quotations credited to Alice Meynell on p. 4, for example, were attributed by him to 'V. M. (of Swinburne)' and 'Viola Meynell'; but the sense of both, if not the wording, conforms closely to sentences written by Viola Meynell's mother, Alice (for this information we are grateful to Mr. P. M. Fraser). In this case we thought it best to leave unaltered the misquotations – if that is what they are.

The present selection differs from the earlier one in that though the headings of the various sections are taken from the original Notebooks, not every section is substantially represented. Thus only two items from many transcribed by Madan under the heading 'Poetry' are included, and these are inserted under other headings; the same is true of a section in the Notebooks entitled 'Words and Mottoes'; while A. C. Benson, G. K. Chesterton, and G. M. Young, each of whom had a section to himself, are here grouped, together with quotations from other talkers and writers, under the heading

'Extracts and Summaries' – as is also the section devoted to Madan's own phrases and reflections. In the original Notebooks, 'Extracts and Summaries' included many long quotations from Henry James. Madan's sympathetic admiration of James's writings is an essential feature of the portrait that we have attempted to sketch; and it was in that rich mine of images and metaphors that Marjorie found the phrase so exactly applicable to her husband: 'the elegant complicated medal struck off for a special occasion'.

We cannot conclude this Introduction without an acknowledgment of our particular gratitude to Mr. Richard Brain for the help he has given us in our work upon the book. Not only did Mr. Brain encourage us to undertake a selection from Madan's Notebooks and suggest that we should submit it to the Oxford University Press, of which he was then a member, but at every stage he has supplied us so readily with advice and practical assistance that we have come to regard him almost as a fellow-editor.

We are grateful also to Geoffrey Madan's sister, Mrs. C. G. Brocklebank, and his daughter, Lady Campbell of Croy, for much indispensable information.

Finally, we tender our warmest thanks to Mr. Harold Macmillan for contributing as a Foreword his appreciative reminiscence of his friend.

J.A.G.
J.S.

The gold of that land is good: there is bdellium and the onyx stone.

Genesis 2:12

BEAUTY, POINT, AND CHARM

Note in Gladstone's Dante (which I saw at the Rosebery sale) on '*Nel mezzo del cammin* . . . ':*15–49* [*years old*].

Theory of laughter as 'superior adaptation'.

Ludovici

A single villa can mar a landscape, and dethrone a dynasty of hills.

Ruskin

I hate false words, and seek with care, difficulty, and moroseness for those that fit the thing.

Landor

The successors of the Tsars of Russia could hardly be expected to value a sacred manuscript: but the knowledge that such things have a price was fortunately brought to their notice.

The Times *on the Codex Sinaiticus*

Sir George Lewis invited every year to Balmoral: never accepting.

He was unlike a man in many things, and like the schoolmaster abroad in others.

E. F. Benson, of the Prince Consort

The House of Lords *should* be an irrationally constituted body, like a jury.

D. B. Somervell

Two impressions remaining, after a life of scientific research:
1. The inexhaustible oddity of nature.
2. The capacity of the human system for recovery.

J. B. S. Haldane

I belong to the generation that says goodbye at the front door.

Max Beerbohm

Distinction between asking 'How is your brother?' and saying 'I hope your brother is well', laid down in manual of etiquette (1860).

A chaos of clear ideas.

Faguet, of Voltaire's philosophy

'With people like you, love only means one thing.'
'No, it means twenty things: but it doesn't mean nineteen.'

Arnold Bennett's Journal

Lord Oxford died *downstairs* at the Wharf, in the black 'Bridge' room.

Sir Roderick Meiklejohn (22 February 1933)

1. The 'affected smartness' of the chapter-heading 'Outside Dorl-cote Mill'.
2. The absolutely shocking introduction of sarcasm.
3. The pertness of her reflexions: due in large measure to the influence of Mr. Ruskin.

Quarterly Review *on George Eliot (1860)*

Where pattering acorns *oddly* drop.

John Clare

The lines in a stanza of Spenser, like bars of gold thrown ringing one upon another.

W. B. Yeats

George has introduced me to an American. I like him in a moderate way. I told him I hated Englishmen because they were the only men I knew. He does not understand this.

Keats, 31 January 1820

Mrs. Yates Thompson told me that she crossed the Channel with Ruskin on a rough day: he recommended *jumping* as a cure for sea-sickness.

' . . . for it's there they cleaned their ships, sir, asking your pardon.'
R. L. Stevenson, Treasure Island, *Ch. 12. W. P. Ker*
and A. E. Housman pointed out that the natural word
would have been 'bottoms'

Harnack thought *Hebrews*
Professor Bacon thought *Revelation* } were written by women.

He was not afraid of conversation.

The Times *obituary of Spooner*

A. J. Balfour not forgetting having been Home Secretary but remembering having been, when he never was.

When the Church neglects a duty, a sect springs up:
    Anointing of sick: Christian Science
    Prayers for the dead: Spiritualism
    Confession: Psycho-analysis
(What had the Jews neglected, to get Christianity?)

Vice, being hard, can take a polish too.
Line praised by Newman in The Oxford Spy *(James Boone)*

Lord Chatham reading Shakespeare to his family aloud, but when he came to the comic parts, handing the book to his son.

45,000 copies of Morley's *Life of Gladstone* sold on day of publication, at 2 guineas each.
Harold Macmillan told me this (June 1931)

The real truth is that Tennyson . . . is deficient in intellectual power.
Matthew Arnold

Archbishop of Canterbury on Council of Board of Trade till 1882, and receiving notices of meetings till 1911: still invited to yearly dinner.

Un homme pénétrant aurait pu annoncer dès le samedi que Jésus revivrait.
Renan

On eût fort étonné ce Jérémie si on lui eût dit que le péché des autres ne le regardait pas.

Anatole France

Odd that we call the end of a rope or a chain, the *end*; while in Greek it is the *beginning*.

Peel's smile: like the silver plate on a coffin.

O'Connell

He kept, as it were, a harem of words, to which he was constant and absolutely faithful. Some he favoured more than others, but he neglected none. He used them more often out of compliment than of necessity.

Alice Meynell, of Swinburne

Children who are *cool* in cold weather.

Alice Meynell

A 'Collins', really a letter *suggesting* a visit.

Clamorous owl that hoots at our quaint spirits.
Keats's note in his copy of Shakespeare, referring to Dr. Johnson

Lord Esher told me in 1927 that when he stayed at Chatsworth as a boy about 1860 there were no bells, but knots of footmen stood about in the passages day and night. The marks of powdered wigs were visible on the walls where they leant back.

Thomas Hardy told me in 1915 that Max Gate was simply 'Mac's gate'; an old turnpike kept by a Scotchman.

Herbert Gladstone told me at Hawarden (September 1928) that Mr. Gladstone never wore the 'Gladstone' collar of today; the band was always two inches wide, a fashion still worn by Tyrolese peasants.

Bradbury, owner of *Punch*, allows no allusion to *death* in the paper: reads all proofs, etc., censored story of little girl saying, 'Not twins, what's left of triplets.'

> *Told me by Sir Lawrence Jones [1857–1954]. (I asked Owen Seaman about this, 19 December 1933. He said the tradition was based on the accident of the Balfour cartoon. [18 June 1892, with a skeleton and the caption 'Dissolution causes gloom over the London scene.'])*

Mme du Deffand's most contented reflection in old age: the thought that she was *not* married to M. de Jonzac.

Ignatius Dark: name of sexton at Cam who helped my grandfather [the Revd. George Madan] in 1832 to bury parishioners who had died of cholera.

Lench and Dummer: boys in *Vice Versa* who only appear once. Also Ing and Pickstones (porters).

Brougham in 1816 moving that the records of income tax should be destroyed, in order to protect posterity even from hearing of it.

1. Disraeli, like a conjuror on a platform.
2. A feeling as though the air was fanned by invisible wings. (Of Gladstone's oratory)

> *Curzon*

Duke of Wellington disapproved of soldiers cheering, as too nearly an expression of opinion.

In the sad hour when summer's cup is full.

> *Edward Shanks*

Taste after taste upheld with kindliest change (*Paradise Lost*, v. 336). Note in Tennyson's copy: *French cook*.

View from Westminster Bridge is North and South: Croydon visible in distance.

If you are ever at a loss to support a flagging conversation, introduce the subject of eating.

Leigh Hunt

Amour: same meaning in Mongolian.

He was worthy of a rare moment.

> The Times *obituary of M. R. James, 13 June 1936. ['He and Dr. Warre, when Provosts of the two foundations in 1910, were allowed to search in St. George's for the uncertain resting place of King Henry's bones, and found them. To Dr. James, who knew better than anyone else every legend, every statue, every portrait of the King, it was a moment of the truest romance when, with his own hands, he reverently wrapped in white silk and reburied those battered, sacred remains. He was worthy of a rare moment.'*]

I know men; and I tell you, Jesus Christ was not a man.

Napoleon at St. Helena

Exclamation mark (!) first used about 1380. Scholiasts say: here the author expresses surprise, etc.

Words without rhymes:
Silver: month: depth: false.

The German accepts an American argument far more readily than a European. He will find the Frenchman too precise, the Englishman too vague and instinctive, the Italian too subtle, the Russian too insincere. The American he at once finds practical and convincing. What the Frenchman would criticize as prolix and hypocritical, he finds full, thorough, and yet adequately idealistic and sentimental. His own thoroughness reconciles him to the method of American biography; and he endures without an anaesthetic the story of the corner block that was bought for $5 by a newsboy, and is now worth a million.

Lord D'Abernon

I do wish Nelson would stop signalling: we all know what to do . . . .

Admiral Collingwood

[Spencer Walpole (1806–98) 'more elegant, fantastical, and interesting than ever, and] he talks of changing his name and retiring to Parma or Cremona, or some other city equally decayed and unvisited. Venice too vulgar, with Monckton Milnes writing sonnets in every gondola, and making every bridge a Bridge of Sighs.'

Letter from Disraeli to his sister, September 1840

Trapping rats, no use: because the adventurous males get caught: the females get a rest, and the race improves.
Emotional reaction of rats in a hopeless position: like children.

Quarterly Review, *October 1942*

Clerk of City Council signs surname only, like a peer: Schuster.

Burke, on the death of his only son, refused a peerage. He would have chosen the title Beaconsfield.

M. R. James: The Bible would take a scribe about 1½ years to copy.

Every schoolboy has the famous testament of Grunius Corocotta Porcellus at his fingers' ends.

Not Macaulay but Burton, Anatomy of Melancholy,
Part 3, Sect. 1, Mem. 1, Subs. 1

Two Archbishops and Bishop of Durham hold office 'by Divine Providence': all others by 'Divine Permission'. Hensley Henson added that some bishops do so by Divine Inadvertence.

Nothing so dreadful as moonlight on a garden wall have I seen . . . but starshine is like carols in heaven at the Nativity.

Burne-Jones [letter to Lady Horner printed in Time Remembered]

Je n'ai fait celle-ci plus longue que parceque je n'ai pas eu le loisir de la faire plus courte.

Pascal [Lettres provinciales, *xvi*]

7

He was a great, perhaps an unconscious, actor. Chance made him an autocrat, and gave him the world for a stage. Only in the last phase of his life, as a self-made recluse, was he able to be his natural self. Then he led a life of dignified seclusion which half redeemed and wholly contradicted his active career. He became indeed a respectable, talented, agreeable, rather vain country gentleman.

Sir Valentine Chirol, of the Kaiser, Quarterly Review,
October 1941

Go in in front of Royalty: but never *pass* in front of them.

Princess Mary (Eton, 18 March 1939)

Use of capitals in referring to God (He, His, etc.) product of 19th-century High Church Romanticism: not found in the 16th or 17th centuries.

Sir Walter Raleigh (1861–1922)

The Wall of China, the only work of man visible from the moon.

Fortnightly Review, *August 1939*

Trafalgar signal: Nelson confides. . . .

HUMOROUS AND MEMORABLE

American politics: dullness, occasionally relieved by rascality.
Sir Cecil Spring Rice

A rose has no back.
Chinese reply if you apologize for turning your back

Arm-in-arm, or otherwise linked together.
*From Vincent Baddeley's circular to female staff at the
Admiralty*

A Lancashire M.P.: 'Liar.'
Under-Secretary: 'My friend is anxious to protect me from what he
thinks is an inaccuracy.'

I was overcome by the resemblance to my sainted Mother: and she
was a very beautiful woman.
Disraeli, canvassing at High Wycombe (A. J. Balfour)

Samuel Butler placing Dante among the Seven Humbugs of the
World solely on the ground that Tennyson admired him.

Oh, a little – in a rough sort of way.
*Bernard Berenson, when I asked if Sir Robert Witt knew
anything about pictures*

Selfridge, when you call, having nothing on his desk except *your*
letter, smoothed and ironed.
Oliver Lyttelton

The Blue Book about Keats.
Robert Ross, of Sir Sidney Colvin's Life

9

Trousers should shiver on the shoe but not break.

Arnold Bennett's tailor

Bookplate of 'Rosebery, 10 Downing Street'.

Truman fiddles while Byrnes roams . . . (Paris, 1946).

Twelve years necessary to undo the harm caused by Housman's lecture on Poetry.

I. A. Richards

'This is not mentioned by the Synoptists, and is passed over by St. John: but full details may be found in Farrar's *Life of Christ*.'

J. L. Joynes [Eton master], wearing a top hat in bed.

The Times, *15 March 1934*

Queen Victoria 'indicating with uplifted fan' that a sermon should stop.

Quarterly Review, *April 1901*

George III not having seen the sea aged 34.

Horace Walpole Memoirs

The sun has risen twice today.

Chinese formula on meeting you unexpectedly

Asquiths in Cavendish Square had 24 servants, who all attended prayers.

Cyril Asquith

St. Joseph's *cigar* in National Gallery Piero della Francesca [*Nativity*].

Episcopal seal of Durham round not oval: i.e. royal.

When Frenchmen are talking, never lift the needle off the gramophone: it only goes back to the beginning.

Oliver Lyttelton

Any stigma is good enough to beat a dogma with.

> *Philip Guedalla*

Smoking forbidden in *stations*.

> *Bradshaw (1839)*

Omlet, Omlet, dies is dein Feyder's spooke.

> *Dutch* Hamlet

Did you have the carriage to yourself?

> *Ordinary question circa 1913*

J. H. S. (Trustee of National Gallery, National Portrait Gallery, etc.) hanging a Cézanne landscape *on its side* for 31 years, as *Reflexions in Water*.

> *O. T. Falk* [? *Of John Hugh Smith, Treasurer and Member of the Executive Committee, National Art Collections Fund*]

Young man charged, after Royal wedding, with tearing a detective's waistcoat to pieces.

Oscar Wilde like a man gorged with grass.

> *Michael Field* [Works and Days, *p. 140:*
> '*There is no charm in his elephantine body, tightly stuffed into his clothes – with a grass-gorged effect*']

U.S.A. won't believe in the brotherhood of man till bombing planes can cross the Atlantic.

Important if true. Inscription which Kinglake wanted on all churches.

Iron railings leaning out of the perpendicular.

> *Palmerston, on Foreign Office handwriting*

Caverne des Grands Voleurs (1783). Original of the Tussaud Chamber of Horrors.

When do children want their birthdays? 'Presently.'

> [*A child's answer to Marjorie Madan*]

Napoleon, 'as fat and round as a china pig'.

> *Sir William Doveton, 1820, who once met him at breakfast at St. Helena*

Roosevelt nearly christened *Isaac*; but his father happened to admire Franklin Delano at the time.

Instead of being arrested, as we stated, for kicking his wife down a flight of stairs and hurling a lighted kerosene lamp after her, the Revd. James P. Wellman died unmarried four years ago.

> *From an American newspaper, quoted by Burne-Jones in a letter to Lady Horner*

I always spell plumb-pudding (so) – I think it sounds fatter and more suetty.

> *Lamb*, Letters

Chaplain of Trinity reading lessons like an animal crying.

> *A. B. Ramsay*

Mr. C. L. Dodgson neither claims nor acknowledges any connexion with any pseudonym or with any book not published under his own name.

> *Printed reply of Lewis Carroll to correspondents*

Lord Curzon. Lady Cynthia could only get some of her friends asked to her wedding by inventing titles for them, Lord Robey, etc.

Dorsetshire rustics, since Hardy, have the insolence of the artist's model.

> *Robert Ross*

Inventions:
Wolsey	Strawberries and Cream
Duc de Richelieu	Mayonnaise
Dean Nowel	Bottled beer

Talleyrand spent an hour every day with his cook.

Henry Yates Thompson in an Old Harrovian list mentioned as having given £38,000 'for the enlargement of Westminster Abbey'.

[Misinterpretation of a donation for a proposed annexe in which to house monuments]

Why is no food blue?

Jane Asquith (aged 7)

Sun sets on 5 May exactly behind the Arc de Triomphe.

Young Woman in a Museum: What's that bird?
W. P. Ker: It's a guillemot.
Y. W.: That's not my idea of a guillemot.
W. P. K.: It's God's idea of a guillemot.

1. A.   See B. A correspondence between two clergymen on Baptism and Regeneration. 1825.
2. ZZ. Genuine will of clergyman, lately deceased, whose son deservedly possesses one of the highest stations in the Church: containing his remarkable apology for adultery. 1750.

First and last entries in British Museum catalogue

The only man on record whose hair turned black in a single night from fearlessness.

H. W. Nevinson, of C. E. Montague [who dyed his grey hair black in order to conceal his age and to join the Army in 1914]

Disraeli never in Ireland: Gladstone once (1877).

He once smoked a cigar; and found it so delicious that he never smoked again.

Sir Leslie Stephen, of Sir James Fitzjames Stephen

My dear, you're the only woman in the world who'd have known the right hat to wear on an occasion like this.

Oscar Wilde, to Mrs. Leverson, on his coming out of prison

Dean Westcott's letter of condolence to Charles Kingsley on a bereavement: 14 pages: only one phrase could be deciphered, apparently 'ungrateful devil'.

Foreigners:
1. Italian who remained silent because it was too cold to take his hands out of his pockets.
2. Two Spaniards who stopped every now and then on a walk, because the whole body was necessary for talking.

Arnold Bennett said to me, the most tremendous compliment ever paid to him was Lord Beaverbrook's saying: 'Arnold, you're a hard man.'

A cold sweet silver life, wrapped round in waves,
Quickened with touches of transporting fear.

Leigh Hunt [*of fish*]

Bishop of Brisbane, leaning over to William Cory: 'Did you ever know Johnson? I always thought him *the* most unpleasant fellow I ever came across.'
Cory: 'I see just what you mean, but I'm not sure it mayn't have been a little exaggerated.'

[*William Cory, who had changed his name from William Johnson*]

Story of Queen Alexandra and Princess Beatrice:
'Did you see anyone in the Park?'
'We met the Devonshires, and recognized them, Ma'am.'

Montagu Norman described by McKenna as an intellectual without an intellect.

Carlyle described the Watts portrait of himself as looking 'like a mad labourer'.

G. W. Lyttelton

The saying that there are two sorts of pedestrians, the quick and the dead, is well matured: but there are also those who choose to be maimed rather than halt.

The Times *leader, April 1933*

Sights of London: the church in Leicester Square where Mme Navarro, between the matinée and evening performances, used to pray to be delivered from the attentions of King Edward VII.

He was advised by a friend, with whom he afterwards lost touch, to stay at the Wilberforce Temperance Hotel.

His son's Life of Lord Birkenhead

In club library: Whisk to dust books in Theological section.

Hallam and Tennyson at meeting of the Apostles (1829), lying on the ground in order to laugh less painfully, when Spedding imitated the sun going behind a cloud and coming out again.

Desmond MacCarthy to me (Garrick Club, June 1943)

Simson: German for Samson in Qld Testament. *Simsons Hochzeit*: *Rache der Delilah gegen Simson*: *Tod des Simson*: *dann sagte Delilah an Simson, Simson was willst du?*

Two anarchists talking: 'What time is it by your bomb?'

God not mentioned in one book only of the Bible: *Esther*.

That was when you were only a worried look on your father's face.

Entertainer at Trocadero

143 French churches were cathedrals before the Revolution.

M. R. James [Eton & King's, 1926, p. 152. M.R.J. claimed to have visited all but two, Nice and Toulon]

PEERS, in House of Lords Library: not GENTLEMEN.

Harold Robson told me (5 February 1943) that he saw the Treaty of Versailles being sealed in a tea-pantry off the Lord Chancellor's office, by a servant, who suggested he should come and have a look.

In a crisis, public or private, their first reaction is to stop thinking: their second, to play a round of golf.

Owen Seaman

Rhodes spending £8,000 on having translations made of all Gibbon's authorities.

The Italian Mission in England.

> *Lord Palmerston, on the Roman Catholic Church*

A face geometrically impossible: the parts were greater than the whole.

> *John Oliver Hobbes*

Names:
Trampleasure: Leatherbarrow: Ballhatchet: Wallcousins: Bullwinkle: Rupert *Chawner* Brooke: Archer Hind: Torn Sibby: Pitblado: Hornbuckle: Portrait: Claringbull:
Ernest Joseph Cassel: Joseph Rudyard Kipling:
Francis Albert Augustus Charles Emmanuel (Prince Consort): Benjamin *Williams* Leader: Arthur Spenser Loat Farquharson: *Teakle* Wallis Warfield: Brownbea: Polyblank: Buttolph: Sir Jholibhoy Alghas.

Man at Tuesday Club: Anyway I'd rather be right than clever.
O. T. Falk: I'd rather be both than neither.

John Morley: as a publisher's reader rejecting *Poems and Ballads* (1866) and *A Shropshire Lad* (1895).

Commander of Russian ship at Naval Review (May 1937) called 'Arch-comrade'.

Salad should be dry and tired: that's the great thing.

> *Heard in Brooks's, 1937*

The Bible:
1. No one coughs. One person sneezes. Only one woman's age is mentioned (Sarah: 127).
2. Cruden left out Buz (brother of Huz): and Sneeze (put under Neeze).

> *The Times, 7, 12, and 20 October 1937*

If you're made a peer, go *up* in the alphabet. (Story of Abbott, who got a cheque from his aunt for being head of a list.)

Campbell-Bannerman

P. H. Shaw-Stewart is the life and soul of the party: – or anyway the *life* of it.

Letter of Rupert Brooke, 1915 (Violet Bonham Carter, 28 October 1941)

'There's only one "aspirated s" in English: the word sugar.'
R. A. Knox: 'Are you *sure*?'

E. F. Benson

I knew it would be dull, but not so dull as this.

Lord Melbourne, of Every Man in his Humour

I cannot see the man for the likeness.

Roger Fry, of Sargent's portrait of Ian Hamilton

Bells in National Club [an evangelical institution]: one ringing next door only, for coffee; one for prayers, on same floor.

Doré:
The whole work of: one slimy efflux of the waters of Styx. p. 4.

Ruskin, Index to Collected Works

Lives in D.N.B.: [of interest and not usually read]

1. T. H. Bayly
2. James Gatliff
3. J. S. Watson
4. Dean Aldrich
5. John Nichols Tom
6. John Howell
7. Antony Addington
8. John Henderson (1757–88)
9. John Marriott (1780–1815)
10. Bishop Charles Lloyd
11. Sir Herbert Croft (1751–1816)
12. Edmund Barker O.T.N. [*]
13. Joshua Barnes
14. Edward Gibbon Wakefield
15. Edward Bradley
16. Benjamin Hawkshaw
17. Elizabeth Bland

[*Of Thetford, Norfolk]

Psalm 46: 46th word SHAKE: 46th word from end SPEAR: Shakespeare 46 in 1611.

Anagrams [selected from among 74]

EVANGELICALISM
1. A call is given me
2. Sing me 'I've a call'
3. Sell naive magic
4. All same vice, gin

LESS FORNICATION . . . ?!
R.C. saint's life? O no!

UNBUSINESSLIKE
i.e. less bunk in us

'MUFTI' – AS IT IS
A 'misfit' suit

AH WHO'S DEAN INGE?
A sane whig don, he

BADGER IN TRAIN
Grin and bear it
[riposte to LION IN TRAM
Trinominal]

SIR BARTLE AND LADY FRERE
Rated rare friends by all
[presented to the Freres on
their wedding anniversary]

WINSTON CHURCHILL
I'll throw Huns' C.-in-C.

PRESBYTERIAN
Best in prayer

ASTRONOMERS
No more stars

R.A.F. CADS BIT TORY PEER
Prefabricated story

RINSE PLEASE
'Ere, less pain

WHY BORSTAL'S IRATE
It's beastly Harrow

VALETUDINARIAN
A nature invalid

AH! SHE'S FIT NOW – REALLY
Sly faith-healer's won!

IN A TOOTHACHE
Oh! Oh! I can't eat

INACTION
I can? Not I

HORATIO NELSON
Honor est a Nilo

REGIMENTAL QUARTERMASTERS
Alert smart square tiger-men

He was a fine old *mouser*!
> *Alexander Day to Northcote, of Titian* [*1779: Hazlitt,*
> Conversations with Northcote]

New English Dictionary originally *A(n) Historical English Dictionary*:
Murray and Bradley unable to agree.

In disease Medical Men guess: if they cannot ascertain a disease,
they call it nervous.

Keats

I never went to the Derby. Once, though, I nearly did : I happened
to be passing through Derby, that very day.

Bishop Westcott

Curious how much more room dirty clothes take up than clean ones,
when you're packing – quite out of proportion to the amount of dirt
they contain.

Claud Russell [*Edward Marsh*, A Number of People, *1939*]

A good deal of the sterilized milk of human kindness in him.

Robert Ross, of Charles Ricketts

So they went forth both, and the young man's dog with them.

Tobit 5:16: *the only mention in the Bible of a pet*
animal

Bethmann-Hollweg in 1914 being made a Colonel, with uniform,
in order to announce declaration of war.

III

ACADEMICA

Praeivit: inscription, 1646, in St. John's College, Oxford.
> ['*He went before*': grave of Nicolas Vilett in Chapel. 'I
> have always understood the meaning of the inscription to
> be that, as an Esquire Bedel, he walked at the head of
> University processions.' A. L. Lane-Poole, President of
> St. John's, 20 December 1948]

The Newcastle is an unsatisfactory examination, spoilt by the
Divinity, which is simply an invention for garrulous and unfastidi-
ous boys.

William Cory

Two Miss Gullivers [Eton 'Dames']. One, totally deaf, remained at
top of house: when informed in writing of disorder, would circulate
port and seed-cake.

Shane Leslie told me this at Eton (1932)

*Magna eloquentia sicut flamma materia alitur et motibus excitatur et urendo
clarescit.*
Pitt's extempore translation, according to story told to Rogers by
Redhead Yorke:
'It is with eloquence as with a flame. It requires fuel to feed it,
motion to excite it, and it brightens as it burns.'

Mrs. Cornish (abstractedly): 'He preaches such wonderful sermons.'
'But, Mrs. Cornish, he doesn't preach sermons: he isn't a clergy-
man.'
Mrs. Cornish: 'Then why drag him into the conversation?'

Provost Hornby, hearing the catechism at Eton, to a boy whose
Christian name was Hyacinth: 'And who gave you *that* name?' with
the faintest perceptible emphasis.

House of Commons quotations (*Classical Review*, July 1932):

1. Declined $\begin{cases} \text{temporarily after 1832.} \\ \text{actually after 1809.} \end{cases}$

2. Concidunt venti fugiuntque nubes . . . .

>> *Quoted by Burke (1775), Fox, Marryat, Lord Lynd-hurst (twice), Huskisson, and Gladstone*

3.   Paribus se legibus ambae
invictae gentes aeterna in foedera mittant.

>> *Quoted by Pitt (1800), Grant, Macaulay, Russell, O'Connell, Brougham, and Palmerston*

4. Instar veris enim . . . .

>> *Lord Portman (1837)*

5. Macaulay never quoted: once repeated a quotation of Pitt.

6. Lord Chatham:
Tuque prior, tu parce, genus qui ducis Olympo.
>> *Of George III as opposed to Lord North*

7. Bright quoted Latin once only: a modern hexameter from the front page of Bagster's Bible:
>> Multi terricolis animi: coelestibus unus.

8. Emicuit Stilichonis apex, et cognita fulsit
canities.
>> *Disraeli on the Duke of Wellington (bagged from Guizot!)*

Nunquam immemores: nunquam satis memores.

> *Stanton Church*

Orbis Britannici Rex.

> *Suggested by Jebb for the coinage*

English describe scenery as if you'd never seen it before: Romans as if they were just reminding you of it.

> *A. B. Ramsay*

Graece vel latrine redditum.

> *British Museum catalogue*

No Greek: as much Latin as you like: never French in any circumstances: no English poet unless he has completed his century.
> *Fox's advice for House of Commons quotations*

Balliol 'Annual Register' written in Latin up till 1914.

Let us emulate the wise and generous tolerance of the sun, which rises over Wadham, and sets over Worcester.

R. A. Knox

Conington's idea of the working classes, said to be 'a large generalization from his scout'.

C. E. V. Buxton's Shakespeare reading for the Cambridge Eight held up by man at Corpus discovered to be unable to read.

D. A. Winstanley

Wavell mi. has done well in Africa.

Summer Fields Magazine

Boys like to be employed: they value praise: many have a strong sense of duty: but almost all dislike thinking.

M. D. Hill [Eton master]

A schoolmaster looks *at* you: a don looks the way you're looking.

Sir Walter Raleigh

Traditional immunity from cannibalism enjoyed by wearers of a Balliol tie.

Lord Elton

New College men, when they read for Greats, start by learning six arguments against Hedonism.

I believe in examinations because I believe in original sin. Boys and girls are full of it, they are lazy, slapdash, etc., and examinations mean doing the best you can with the means at your disposal, all on your own, and against the clock. Examinations are just like life, the only thing almost, that boys and girls do in school that is really like life.

John Murray [1879–1964]

True scholarship lies in the capacity to make a long arm and bring back the relevant observation. That was Bentley. That was not Housman. Nor, quite, Porson. But it was Headlam.

G. M. Young

Vaughan of Harrow:
1. Advice of Vicar of Harrow: dismiss *all* the 69 boys who were left.
2. Locking into vestry a Scotch boy who appeared in a kilt.

Lord Hugh Cecil preaching (Miss Goodford present) and saying that eternal torment was almost certain: but a very few might hope for merciful annihilation.

Eton, 25 November 1944

'Do you know all the boys?'
Warre [Headmaster of Eton]: 'No, no, but they all know *me*.'

C. M. Wells's pupil: 'Sir, when I leave I'm going to do *nothing*.'

What sort of place *is* it, sir? Something in the Keble line?
Raymond Asquith's scout on his return from Cambridge

H. M. Butler: 'Christ, in a very real sense, a Trinity man.'

Dr. Butler at Shrewsbury: 'The melancholy truth stares me in the face.'
[*On reading legend left on blackboard: 'Butler is an ass'*]

Harrow unable to form an Eleven (1941): three boys called up, two interned.

Master of John's, giving fellowships for 'learning' rather than 'godliness': 'With their godliness they may deceive me, with their learning they cannot.'
[*Of Anthony Tuckney, Master 1653–61*]

Boy in C. M. Wells's house, too *busy* to open his parents' letters.

Missionary preacher: 'Of course I was in the Eight and the Eleven, and that sort of thing.'
[*'The statement was true. The laugh was really on the boys who thought it was a boast.' G. W. Lyttelton*]

I have placed your theme, Sir, on the mantelshelf in my nursery, that the children may scoff at it.

G. G. Bradley

Oman, of the Senior Fellow of All Souls in 1883 (elected in 1836): required *only* to write a Latin Essay 'De Maris fluxu et refluxu'.

Lord Hugh Cecil thinking boys should be prepared for confirmation by the chaplain at home.

Finis laborum meorum. . . .

Edmund Warre

['*At the last school, which was a saying lesson, I was the last boy to come up and say my piece and therefore found myself alone with him. When I had done he shut the book with these words: "Finis laborum meorum." This was a terribly impressive moment for me, and I would have given anything to have made a suitable reply, preferably in Latin – but I could think of nothing to say.' Note from Lord Darnley, 11 June 1948*]

Hornby [Headmaster of Eton]: 'I rather wish Shelley had been at Harrow.'

I am free to admit that I have never been one of those who refuse to meet a Cambridge man upon a level of complete social equality.

Warden Brodrick

Ram seems to have lost his head rather.

Lord Cobham at Hagley, 1913 [on a generously worded report by A. B. Ramsay, his son's housemaster at Eton]

Avia Pieridum peragro loca nullius ante trita solo.

Paper-knife at Magdalen [Lucretius, I. 926]

Inventors of words:

Bentham	International
Boyle	intensify, essence [concrete], fluid [noun]
Sir Thomas Browne	precarious, insecurity, medical, literary, electricity, hallucination, antediluvian, incontrovertible
Burke	colonial, diplomacy, financial, expenditure, municipality, representation [political]
Miss Burney	propriety [meaning conformity with good manners]
Byron	bored, blasé
Carlyle	captain of industry, 'message', outcome, decadent
Chaucer	attention, position, duration, fraction
Chesterfield	etiquette, picnic
Coleridge	pessimism, phenomenal, Elizabethan
Cudworth	dramatist, fatality
Eikon Basilike	demagogue
Evelyn	outline, attitude, contour
Hawtrey	deflation
Huxley	agnostic
Dr. Johnson	comic, literature
Macaulay	constituency
Milton	echoing, rumoured, gloom, impassive, liturgical
Henry More	central, circuitous, freakish, fortuitous
Scott	gruesome, stalwart, free-lance, red-handed
Tennyson	fairy tale
Tindale	long-suffering, broken-hearted, scape-goat

APHORISMS AND REFLECTIONS

It requires a penetrating eye to discern a fool through the disguise of gaiety and good breeding.

Fielding

I am always glad when one of those fellows dies, for then I know I have the whole of him on my shelf.

Lord Melbourne, speaking of Crabbe

Life is like playing a solo on the violin, and learning the instrument as you go along.

Samuel Butler

Public schools are to private schools as lunatic asylums to mental homes: larger and less comfortable.

Owen Seaman

To know him was a liberal education: it was also a conservative one.

D. A. Winstanley, of R. V. Laurence (1934)

An able accountant.

Balfour, of McKenna

1. It should be our faith that everything in this world can be expressed in words.
2. It is often genius that spoils a work of art.
3. Owing to their imperfect education, the only works we have had from women have been works of genius.

Oscar Wilde [quoted by Michael Field]

People are entitled to shout when they are drunk. That is not being disorderly.

De Privilegiis Compotandi. (The Magistrate at Clerkenwell:
Mr. Campion)

Levez-vous, Monsieur le Comte, vous avez de grandes choses à faire aujourd'hui.

Valet of Duc de Saint-Simon's nephew

Some people take no mental exercise except jumping to conclusions.

1. Inaccuracy may be voluble, a lie may be glib: but spontaneity is the vesture of truth.
2. We must carefully distinguish between the absence of tact and the presence of principle.
3. Dignity *is* impudence.
4. Logic is the strong delusion which God sends.

John Davidson

My own suspicion is that the universe is not only queerer than we suppose, but queerer than we *can* suppose.

J. B. S. Haldane

Study means unlearning.

Lord Bryce

The riddle of Life is solved by gliding, and not by sliding.

Dream of A. C. Benson

1. Confession is a kind of pride.
2. A diary would have been conversation if it could.
3. Overwork tires: underwork wearies.

Balfour Browne, K.C.

1. If 2 or 3 Englishmen are together any length of time, and do not laugh, something has gone wrong.
2. It is as hard to be humble as it is easy to despair.
3. Bradshaw . . . told me he had never seen a mediaeval library without Valerius Maximus.

William Cory

To be happy in threes is a great test of the capacity for being happy at all.

Mary Coleridge

An Englishman's mind works best when it is almost too late.

Lord D'Abernon

One should not lay stress on the oddities and angularities of great men. They should never be hawked about.

Tennyson, of a story told of Dr. Johnson by Miss Langton, his godchild

Always take out your watch when a child asks you the time.

J. A. Spender

There is no villainy to which education cannot reconcile us.

Trollope

In France, to be a man's man you must first be a woman's man: in England, to be a woman's man you must start by being the other.

What is the use of lying, when truth, well distributed, serves the same purpose?

W. E. Forster

I love fun, but too much is abominable.

Blake

Le premier, embellit; le deuxième, conserve; le troisième – gâte tout.

[*On women's lovers*]

Mr. Gladstone's idea of impartiality is to be furiously in earnest on both sides of a question.

Lord Houghton

1. Never back a friend's bill.
2. Never go to church on the 15th evening of the month.

Lord Salisbury (father of the Prime Minister)

Jamais un homme heureux n'eût inventé la vertu.

Charles Régismanset

Pour goûter pleinement le bonheur, il n'y a rien de tel que d'en être indigne.

Etienne Rey

En amour, les femmes vont jusqu'à la folie, et les hommes jusqu'à la bêtise.

Philippe Gerfaut

Quelle rancune, cette rancune séculaire pour une pomme volée sur un pommier tabou.

L'Amiral Réveillère

Il faut savoir faire les sottises que nous demande notre caractère.

Chamfort

On peut démolir des palais, on ne rasera point les antichambres.

Achille Tournier

La santé est un état fragile, provisoire, et qui ne presage rien de bon.

Une oraison funèbre dit exactement ce que le mort aurait dû être.

Gustave Vapereau

Après la bataille, c'est là que triomphent les tacticiens.

Anatole France

Parmi les livres, il y a aussi de faux amis.

Jean-Philibert Damiron

Avec de l'imagination et des obstacles, on peut toujours adorer une femme: il n'est pas aussi facile de l'aimer.

Alphonse Karr

On a toutes les audaces quand on désire une femme: toutes les timidités quand on l'aime.

Hector Molot

Le divorce est à peu près de même date que le mariage: je crois que le mariage est de quelques semaines plus ancien.

Voltaire

Le bon sens et le génie sont de la même famille; l'esprit n'est qu'un collatéral.

Les gens faibles sont les troupes légères de l'armée des méchants.

Chamfort

L'orgueil des petits consiste à parler toujours de soi: l'orgueil des grands est de n'en parler jamais.

Voltaire

On tient à l'éloge et aux honneurs dans l'exacte mesure où l'on n'est pas sûr d'avoir réussi.

Bergson

On ne peut jamais bien corriger son ouvrage qu'après l'avoir oublié.

Voltaire

L'amour est une colonie de soi-même que l'on pense avoir dans le coeur choisi.

Paul Hervieu

Il ne faut pas croire que toutes les marques de confiance soient des marques d'amitié.

Abbé Brueys

Cette effroyable patience de l'ambition, qui se couche plus tard que le vice, et se lève plus tôt que la vertu.

Auguste Filon, of Prosper Mérimée

Il existe de services si grands qu'ils ne peuvent se payer que par l'ingratitude.

Alexandre Dumas

L'exquis de l'élégance est de fixer l'attention sans l'attirer.

Hippolyte Taine

Il me semble voir dans une pharmacie homéopathique le protestant-isme de la médecine.

Edmond and Jules de Goncourt

Il en coûte cher pour être raisonnable: il en coûte la jeunesse.

Mme de la Fayette

La superstition est l'écume de la foi, et le matérialisme la lie de la libre pensée.

Gustave Vapereau

There is no bore like a brilliant bore.

Samuel Butler

Humility is the only virtue that schoolboys demand of one another.

Edward Lyttelton

I always tell a young man not to use the word 'always'.

Robert Walpole

Shakespeare should never be mentioned with an epithet.

Mrs. Trench (1815)

1. A fellowship is the grave of learning.
2. The librarian who reads is lost.

Mark Pattison

What is valuable on such occasions is a *dull friend*.
Bulwer Lytton, to Disraeli when attacked about his speech on the Duke of Wellington

Political Economy: the rich man's version of the Sermon on the Mount.

No good story is quite true.

Leslie Stephen [Life of Milton: D.N.B.]

Slowness is not the same thing as gentleness.

Florence Nightingale

Horse-sense is something a horse has that prevents him betting on people.

Father Mathew

Good people are not so good as they imagine: and bad people are not so bad as the good suppose.

Bishop Creighton (to Lord Acton)

1. Hard work: saying yes or no on insufficient information.
2. His least superficial quality was his frivolity, which sinks to a considerable depth (Eugène Sue).

Lord Bowen

It is in the nature of a work of art to speak ambiguously, like an oracle.

Max Friedländer

Nothing is more difficult than to be at the same time conspicuous and respectable.

Anon: 1830

Take an uncollegiate Englishman, and you will generally find that he has no *friends*.

Bagehot

The applause of all but very good men is no more than the precise measure of their possible hostility.

Canon Liddon

Homer's evidence about what Homer meant cannot be disproved.

Jebb v. Schliemann

A translator should not lackey by his author, but mount up beside him.

Dryden

Bury the carcass of friendship: it is not worth embalming.

Hazlitt

An invitation is the sincerest form of flattery.

A. J. A. Symons

English conversationalists have a miraculous power of turning wine into water.

Oscar Wilde (quoted by Charles Ricketts)

If you believe in episcopacy, it doesn't much matter what else you believe or disbelieve in.

Hastings Rashdall (quoted by A. C. Headlam)

There's a little touch of vulgarity in the thought of any reward – for anything, ever.

William Cory

Consistency is a puerile temptation.

Lord Acton

Prime Ministers, nowadays, are too busy to do much harm.

E. Hilton Young

I have the very highest opinion of scandal. It is founded on the most sacred of things – that is, Truth, and it is built up by the most beautiful of things – that is, Imagination.

[*W. H. Mallock*, The New Republic, *Book IV, Chapter II*]

1. Americans are either wild or dull.
2. If you're given champagne at lunch, there's a catch somewhere.

Lord Lyons

The first thing people do when they've lost all their money is to get themselves photographed, singly and in groups.

Ella Hayter [*G. M.'s aunt*]

He has grown grey in the service of art, and now he grows purple in its disservice.

D. S. MacColl [*of J. S. Sargent? Graham Reynolds has suggested that the remark might have been made of J. B. Manson (1879–1945)*]

My sad conviction is that people can only agree about what they're not really interested in.

Bertrand Russell, New Statesman, *1 July 1939*

I simply ignored an axiom.

Einstein, on Relativity

Treat a work of art like a prince: let it speak to you first.

Schopenhauer

You can always live on what you've got. I do not speak without experience.

Bishop Westcott

Newman . . . wanted to prove that the Church of England was Protestant before the Reformation and Catholic after it.

Maitland

V

PHRASES AND DESCRIPTIONS

Lazards: business *sub specie Universitatis.*

Arthur McDowall

Haldane's urbane voice that carried his words as it were on a salver.

H. G. Wells

The string of lethargic race-horses on which he so robustly plunged: and the bookmakers with their shining morning faces.

Lord Birkenhead, of Lord Dufferin (The Times)

That world which the Peace cannot give.

[Dean Inge?]

His advice was of the kind that is taken.

The Times, of Lord Dawson of Penn

He talks of Church affairs as a retired business-man talks of stocks and shares.

Of Archbishop Fisher (1944)

High, confused sea.

[Nautical expression in log books]

[Miss —— has a forehead like a Siamese kitten and a] mouth like a galosh.

[Mrs. Patrick Campbell, of a rival actress]

In the pages of Pater, the English language lies in state.

George Moore

Not to have been, by instinctive election, on the right side, is to have failed in life.

Pater, Marius the Epicurean

The robust title of occupancy.

Blackstone

Income tax raised to the more convenient figure of 5/–.

Budget, *1937*

Nailing one's colours to the fence.

Harry Cust [*c. 1904, on A. J. Balfour's ambiguous*
attitude to Chamberlain's Protectionist crusade]

The casual impurities of intellectual life: pedantry, hurry, irrelevance, pretentiousness, cleverness.

H. W. Garrod

That capacity for the cool adjustment of two dissimilar things which makes a spark, and is called wit.

Lord Esher, of Lord Rosebery

Not stupid exactly, but . . . cautious in rather a stupid way.

John Thomasson

1. Entitled to bleat B.A. after their names.
2. Institutions, becoming a kind of corporate cad.

D. S. MacColl

Dr. Parr [of himself]: 'inflicting his eye' on a man.

Recorded by De Quincey

The fine full tones of the unembarrassed English, speaking to their equals.

Kipling

He talks of divinity as a clergyman talks of geology.

Newman, of Gladstone

He was always full grown: he had neither the promise, nor the awkwardness, of a growing intellect.

> *S. T. Coleridge, of Pitt,* Morning Post *(1800)*

The room rose with a sort of feathered, silken thunder.

> *B. R. Haydon [of the Coronation of George IV]*

Sir Hugh Walpole: like a friendly pike.

> *Maugham*

He knows everything, except what's good and bad.

> *Of Edward Marsh*

I have had pleasure in exchanging minds with you.

> *Routh, to Lord Campbell*

He spoke as if preaching earnestly, and also hopelessly, on the weightiest things.

> *Carlyle, of Coleridge, in* John Sterling

1. Mrs Browning: curls like the pendent ears of · a water-spaniel, and poor little hands – so thin that when she welcomed you she gave you something like the foot of a young bird.
2. Thackeray: like a colossal infant.
3. Trollope: voice like two people quarrelling.
4. Meredith: play-acting voice: talk like a man dictating to a secretary.

> *Frederick Locker-Lampson*

He has joined what even he would admit to be the majority.

> *John Sparrow [on the death of a supporter of Proportional Representation]*

VI

EXTRACTS AND SUMMARIES

CYRIL ASQUITH

The name 'Sligger' suggesting not a golf club, or a cue rest, but some instrument of a dentist: like a small chopper, with a crank appendage.

> [*According to Cyril Bailey* (F. F. Urquhart, *1936, p. 25) the nickname was probably acquired at a Minehead reading-party in 1892. Originally 'the sleek one'*]

At the 'top of the tree' in every profession we find a sort of congested arboreal slum of Balliol men.

Diana Manners has no heart, but her brains are in the right place.

On Kitchener, at Walmer (1914): cheeks like a map of the Polish railway system.

It was indeed an ironical fate that reserved the simple majesty of a death in battle for this infinitely complex and civilized, scornful and sophisticated being.

> [*Of Raymond Asquith, in J. A. Spender and Cyril Asquith*, Life of H. H. Asquith]

Fighting barbarians in the company of bores and bounders (1914).

Somewhere in the limbo which divides perfect sobriety from mild intoxication.

Limpid, Satanic fluency.

> *Of J. M. Keynes*

Civil servants, like women after a change of life, no longer tempestuous but sapless.

Kitchener: unexpected style: 'shell-torn' craters: not just stabbing soldierly sentences like 'The men are splendid.'

> ['*Kitchener came into Downing Street with the text of the Guildhall speech in his hand which had been prepared for him by the War Office very well, with short, stabbing, soldierly sentences into which he most unexpectedly wanted to introduce journalese, like "shell-torn".' Lady Violet Bonham Carter*]

Donald Somervell: . . . d'you see my point?
C.A.: I don't see your point: but I remember what you said.
> (*17 December 1941*)

Winston Churchill never in love with anyone; except himself, and possibly Clementine.

I'm just going to take a pure stimulant.

> *Of Bovril*

Every one of the doctors has said, or has had to admit . . .
> *Summing-up, 16 March 1943*

Lord Hewart: an average first-class man.

Winston Churchill, after brandy, like a *tortoise*.

Everyone in this country is assumed to know the law: – except the judiciary, who are subject to appeal.

The blast-area round club-bores.

Mrs. Simpson: half governess, half *earwig*.

H. H. Asquith's cabinet reports adjusted to the receptivity of the sovereign.

Winston Churchill's hair (1904) the colour of a bronze putter.

F. E. Brightman (1913): a gamboge-coloured dwarf: a sort of black collar-stud.

Simon: reptilian good-fellowship. A head like a hive.

A. D. Lindsay: face like a butcher.

H. H. ASQUITH

'Why did you murder those workmen at Featherstone in 1893?'
'It was not 1893: it was in '92.'

Reading Mons telegram twice: no other sign of emotion: 'I suppose you're doing everything that's possible.'

Nothing to grease the financial wheels: unless indeed the dust of controversy can be called a lubricant.

Peculiar grasp of a port-glass.

[*Between first and second fingers*]

MARGOT ASQUITH

Genius closely allied to sanity.

Emotional groundswell of really good conversation.

He was the man to point out, with detachment and precision, the line of least resistance.

Lord Birkenhead is very clever, but sometimes his brains go to his head.

'Do you believe in ghosts?'
'Well, appearances are in their favour.'

Academy pictures: of oranges on piano stools, or lobsters on newspapers.

Alfred Lyttelton always had his arm round your waist and his eye on the clock.

Many qualities, but no quality: a prose mind, though its ardour prevented it from being commonplace.

Of Curzon

Figure like someone shot out of a cannon.

[*Of a woman arriving suddenly at a party, all smiles and spangles*]

General Dawes, an imitation rough diamond.

Business men: dull as fish on grass.

French is spoken in every language.

Virginal faces, hard as gongs.

Without stealing the picture, she takes the colour out of it.

Ettie is an *ox*: she will be made into Bovril when she dies.

[*Of Lady Desborough*]

The Bible tells us to forgive our enemies; not our friends.

Governess, about the height of a tennis-net.

Gladstone, not exactly lacking a sense of humour, but not often in the mood to be amused.

Forehead like a knee.

A. C. BENSON

On first meeting me: 'Let me tell you . . . I should have been a good *stockbroker*.'

Trinity dons in Hall looking less where they shall sit than where they shall *not* sit.

Dyer [Eton master], on missing an easy putt: 'I had the sun in my eyes; – and then I have such light eyelashes.'

Portrait like a cheese, with points and cracks of green, and putrescent hands. Lips drawn up like a trumpet; every rift loaded with coaldust.

Objecting to being prayed for : like someone saying, 'I shall mention your name to the Prime Minister when I next see him.'

A strong case, tellingly put.

> *Story of H. M. Butler, Master of Trinity, waking up at*
> *a College meeting*

Percy Lubbock sate like a sheep turned over for shearing.

Warre's fingers, soft and firm, squared by contact with one another, like Cambridge sausages.

Walter Pater's trousers, cut for a man *sitting*, in cubes, and straightened out on rising.

G. T. Lapsley's bedroom, like an operating theatre, with things in jars, copper tubing, syringes and drenches.

Insects, when a stone was lifted, boiling away.

A weeping eye and a moustache that seemed to have spread and taken root again.

Confirmation at Eton: like a huge garden party, faintly overshadowed by a sense of religion.

Charles Sayle's food oppressive: making one feel like the fish that swallowed a piece of money.

E. L. Vaughan's inky claret, revealing at the bottom of the decanter not ordinary lees of wine but insects clasped in some horrible embrace.

Oscar Browning's face, loosely moulded out of dough, smeared with train oil; a climbing, upturned face.

Bishop waking at Athenaeum; first lying purple and distended, then staring, chuckling and winking.

Preacher's mouth apparently crammed with dough or fish.

Boys only show gravity when *you* talk of serious faults, or when *they* talk of athletics.

Archbishop Frederick Temple bowing to royalty: 'all his back, like the back of a bullock, lay beneath me while he shook hands.'

E. F. Benson never lived his life at all; only stayed with it and lunched with it.

The doctrine of omnipotence means that life is a sham fight with evil.

Stephen Phillips as crammers' coach: what subject? 'God forgive me: it was military history,' and he turned on me a solemn eye, in which there was no laughter.

Mrs. Cornish to H. E. Luxmoore saying, 'You will have been feeling more bitterly than any of us that Edward [Austen] Leigh's obituary should have been written by an Old Etonian *flâneur*.' H.E.L. looked grim, seemed to swallow something in his throat, and went away murmuring; came back an hour later, his mouth drawn from ear to ear, to confess that he had written it.

Miss M. [Cordelia Marshall?] sunburnt, as if head and neck had been cut off, filled with vermilion, and replaced.

Mrs. Cornish ordering a cab on an April day 'between the showers': no fixed time.

Robert Bridges's anthology [*The Spirit of Man*]: a vomit after a rich meal.

46

[Eton] masters asleep during Essay in various abandoned attitudes. Hornby like a frozen mammoth in a cave; Stone drooping; Vaughan like a monarch taking his rest; Churchill like a fowl on a perch with a film over his eyes.

Nicholson's portrait: startled, hostile, piggish.

> [*William Nicholson's portrait of A. C. B., painted in 1924 and now in the Fitzwilliam Museum*]

Missionary bishop, like a man roused from a nap on a sofa: head and hair like the husk of a coconut.

Man at dinner, looking as if praying to be supported through a great trial.

E. F. Benson's idea of a good conversation: when neither party remembers a word of what was said afterwards.

F. W. Bussell, elaborately civil, slightly simpering, slightly giggling, impetuous, humorous, ironical, petting, caressing manner.

H. H. Asquith: a cross between a Dissenting Minister and a seller of marine stores.

Duke of Cambridge, at Hagley, after family prayers, hands on knees: 'A damned good institution.'

Moustache like a toothbrush forced through with blows of a hammer.

Hua [French master at Eton] and Warre could neither pronounce the other's name, but each made the same sound in the attempt.

. . . and the Holy Ghost came down on purpose.

> *Supposed description of Monica Grenfell's confirmation in Lady Desborough's* Pages from a Family Journal

I wrote him a careful letter.

47

Frank Lace, never seen to go out; sitting in a kind of porter's chair with a wickerwork hood; reading Bradshaw and planning elaborate cross-country journeys; never speaking, but in the evening retailing the more incautious things said by the younger members of the family. A slice of sponge-cake kept under a bell-glass on his table, and eaten at the stroke of twelve.

BISMARCK

Universal Suffrage: government of a house by its nursery. But you can do anything with children if you only play with them.

Never ill: but once lost a tooth, biting through the hind leg of a hare.
'*O mon Dieu, mon Dieu*': M. de Courcel

Drank champagne out of bottle, to preserve the ethers.

Prussia needs only one ally: the German people.

Princess Marie Louise told me that Bismarck's voice was very soft and expressive.

VIOLET BONHAM CARTER

Letter of H. H. Asquith, undated, about politics etc.: ending, 'so glad you are now old enough to do up your own gaiters'.

Time wives struck out boldly for themselves and stayed at home.

Winston Churchill's appeal to the House of Commons like saying 'Do you love me?' – quite useless.
[*1915, on his leaving office*]

He never eats his words to save his face.

Of Winston Churchill

No loyalty – therefore no rancour.

Of Lloyd George

Mentally *in*adequate women must be Mother Earth, serenity.

On parlour-games at Panshanger: you have to go out of the room, and then come in and pretend to break off your engagement on the telephone.

F. H. BRADLEY

What I like about France is the clear unflinching recognition by everybody of his own luck.

The cost of a thing is the amount of what I call life which has to be exchanged for it, immediately or in the long run.

Every friendship rests on some particular apotheosis of oneself.

If what offends you in general attracts you in one, it is time to trust in Providence.

G. K. CHESTERTON

A man can no more possess a private religion than he can possess a private sun and moon.

To love anything is to see it at once under lowering clouds of danger.

Democracy means giving a vote to your groom: tradition means giving a vote to your grandfather.

The Christian ideal has not been tried and found wanting. It has been found difficult and left untried.

The materialist has a superstition against believing in ghosts.

People who make history know nothing about history. You can see that in the sort of history they make.

It is a fine thing to forgive your enemies: but it is a finer thing not to be too eager to forgive yourself.

. . . you *can* eat your wedding-cake and have it.

We talk of people not knowing the ABC of a subject: but the trouble is they often know the XYZ of it, without the ABC.

WINSTON CHURCHILL

He sat like the great Judge he was, hearing with trained patience the case deployed on every side . . . and when at the end . . . he summed up, it was rarely that the silence he had observed till then, did not fall on all.

Of Asquith, in Great Contemporaries

He presents to me in those red years the same mental picture as a great surgeon before the days of anaesthetics, versed in every detail of such science as was known to him: sure of himself, steady of poise, knife in hand, intent upon the operation: entirely removed in his professional capacity from the agony of the patient, the anguish of relations, or the doctrines of rival schools, the devices of quacks, or the first-fruits of new learning. He would operate without excitement, or he would depart without being affronted; and if the patient died, he would not reproach himself.

Of Haig, in Great Contemporaries

A. P. Herbert's maiden speech: a brazen hussy of a speech.

Neville Chamberlain and Attlee: like a snake fascinating a rabbit? No: a rabbit eating a lettuce.

Be honest. Be just. He has a difficult task. He is in search of a man with talents even more inconspicuous than his own.

Of Stanley Baldwin

Are we to be at the mercy of negro women scrabbling with their toes in the mud of the Zambesi?

On Gold (O. T. Falk)

There but for the grace of God, goes God.

Of Sir Stafford Cripps

(a) Speech which seemed to proceed by a succession of after-thoughts.
(b) A raw and rowdy undersecretary whom the nakedness of the land and the jealousies of his betters have promoted to leadership.
Unused phrases preserved by Edward Marsh

A be-whiskered ecclesiastic, and a certain General Plastiras. I hope his feet are not of clay.

CONFUCIUS

If this is to be borne, *anything* can be borne.
When Hsi-tsui had eight rows of dancers in his house

To give, and yet to do so in a grasping way; that is to be a mere official.

COMTESSE DIANE
Diane de Suin, later Comtesse de Beausacq (1829–1899)

Tout être aimé qui n'est pas heureux paraît ingrat.

Qui se défie, a été trompé – ou trompeur.

La jeunesse dure bien plus longtemps que ne le croient ceux qui sont jeunes.

D'abord on n'aime plus: longtemps après on arrive à n'aimer pas.

Pour plaire aux autres, il faut prendre la peine d'admirer les qualités qu'ils prennent la peine de feindre.

La gaieté bête fait plus qu'ennuyer les gens d'esprit: elle les attriste.

Les belles dents rendent gaie.

Les vertus sont soeurs: les vices sont camarades.

DISRAELI

Men destined to the highest places should beware of badinage.

Grief is the agony of an instant: the indulgence of grief the blunder of a life.

Next to knowing when to seize an opportunity, the most important thing in life is to know when to forgo an advantage.

A fear of becoming ridiculous is the best guide in life.

Dead, but in the Elysian fields.

Of the House of Lords

Oh, the finishing governess.

Of John Stuart Mill

Never complain; never explain.

Something unpleasant is coming when men are anxious to tell the truth.

(Power and fame, without love) at best but jewels set in a coronet of lead.

The art of conversation is to be prompt without being stubborn, to refute without argument, and to clothe grave matters in a motley garb.

I hate men who have always got an answer. There is no talking commonsense with them.

It is rather difficult to work on the feelings of a man who has no heart.

There is nothing like a fall in Consols to bring the blood of English people into cool order. It is your grand state medicine.

An aristocracy is rather apt to exaggerate the qualities and magnify the importance of a plebeian leader. They do this both from generosity and from a natural feeling of self-love.

In England, when a new character appears in our circles, the first question always is: who is he? In France it is: what is he?

Men should always be difficult. I can't bear men who come and dine with you when you want them.

Christianity is completed Judaism, or it is nothing.

Ceremony, enthusiasm, and free speculation are the characteristics of the three great parties in the church.

The high style of conversation . . . ceased with Johnson and Burke. There is no mediocrity in such discourse: no intermediate characters between the sage and the bore.

At a practised crisis I permit them to see conviction slowly stealing over me.
Of deputations

(Memory of early friendships) . . . which softens the heart, and even affects the nervous system of those who have no hearts.

In the Lower House, 'Don Juan' may perhaps be our model: in the Upper House, 'Paradise Lost'.

An insular country, subject to fogs and with a powerful middle class, requires grave statesmen.

The mystery of mysteries is to view machinery making machinery.

You don't have recourse to extraordinary measures when your house is on fire, you adopt ordinary measures: you send for the parish engine.
Of Ireland, 1849

The Duke of Burlington . . . involuntarily reminds you of youth, as an empty orchestra does of music.

The great Apollo of aspiring understrappers, [you have] the smartness of an attorney's clerk, and the intrigue of a Greek of the Lower Empire . . . . The leader of the Whig opposition was wont to say that your Lordship reminded him of a favourite footman on easy terms with his mistress.

Of Palmerston, in Letters of Runnymede

Peace, I hope, with honour.

After the Congress of Berlin in 1878

He was not an intellectual Croesus, but his pockets were full of sixpences.

. . . the agony of precise conceptions.

A maiden speech so inaudible that it was doubted whether after all the young orator really did lose his virginity.

Disraeli was baptized at St. Andrew's, Holborn, in 1817, by the Revd. J. Thimbleby.

I never contradict. I never deny. But I sometimes forget.

Melancholy, after a day of action, is the doom of energetic celibacy.

A 'confident hope' is, at the best, but the language of amiable despair.

One cannot ask any person to meet another in one's own house, without going through a sum of moral arithmetic.

A treeless Capua.

Of Brighton, 1877

RICHARD DUPPA

The great art of a quack is to time his imposture.

All pleasures that sink deep into the heart are tinged with melancholy.

GEORGE ELIOT

Worldly faces never look so worldly as at a funeral.

The elements of kindness and self-indulgence are hard to distinguish in a soft nature.

H. S. FOXWELL

People who carry capitalism so far as to regard high wages as something like a bad harvest.

Economic Journal 46, Dec.1936, p.592

W. E. GLADSTONE

. . . to recreate, among the Anglican clergy, the pure heroic type.

Occupied 18,000 columns of Hansard in his life, and appears in 366 volumes.

Compassion for the poor man is a very fine feeling, and I should be very sorry to say anything that appeared to depreciate, or to undervalue, so sacred a sentiment. But I must say that it is entirely out of place here.

Speech on the Commercial Treaty of 1860

Our first site in Egypt, be it acquired by larceny, or by emption, will be the almost certain egg of an African Empire.

On Christmas Eve, 1869, in a lonely Derbyshire manor, two brothers dined together. Feelings ran high over a disputed inherit-ance, and the younger brother (after securing the connivance of the butler with a bribe) assaulted the elder, doing him grievous bodily harm. He was committed for trial, but released on bail. On the advice of his solicitors, he jumped his bail and fled the country.

Mr. Gladstone, who was much struck by the story, immediately remarked the following seven points as 'especially worthy of attention':

1. The sacredness of the season.
2. The close relationship of the parties.
3. The peculiar violence of the assault.
4. The subornation of the major-domo.
5. The assailant's singular ignorance of the gross illegality of his action.
6. The faulty advice tendered by his attorney.
7. The forfeiture of his recognizances to the Crown.

A. C. Benson

What I undertook was this: to place the Bill in the forefront of the sessional programme. Surely the Hon. Member is not unaware that the forefront is a line, and not a point.

J. A. Spender

Hearing Duke of Wellington saying 'Ha' (1836): a convenient *suspensive* expression.

Indifference to the world is not love of God.

At Hagley (1892): interruption: pointing like a *dagger*, without stopping speech.

HAZLITT

Envy has a mixture of the love of justice in it.

I have known a person who could scarcely open his mouth without offending someone, merely because he harboured no malice in his heart. Thoughtless good-humour will often make more enemies than deliberate spite, which is on its guard and strikes with caution and safety.

The contempt of a wanton for a man who is determined to think her virtuous, is perhaps the strongest of all others.

Cowardice is not synonymous with prudence. It often happens that the better part of discretion is valour.

SIR ARTHUR HELPS (1813–1875)

There is nothing so easily made offensive as good reasoning.

Do not be much surprised at the ingratitude of those to whom you have given nothing but money.

Never make a god of your religion.

Genius is a guide: talent, a leader.

Alas, it is not the child but the boy that generally survives in a man.

Sooner than become beautiful, a man would choose to become a very handsome likeness of his former self.

No one ever praised two men equally, and pleased them both.

How often we should stop in the pursuit of folly, if it were not for the difficulties that beckon us onward.

A. E. HOUSMAN

Hurry me, Nymphs, O, hurry me
Far above the grovelling sea,
Which, with blind weakness and bass roar
Casting his white age on the shore,
Wallows along that slimy floor;
With his widespread webbèd hands
Seeking to climb the level sands,
But rejected still to rave
Alive in his uncovered grave.
                                        (George Darley)

The man who wrote this had seen the sea, and the man who reads it sees the sea again.

Room: lunch of potted meat and biscuits: *jar* of ink on desk.

Found by A. B. Ramsay at 3.30 on a Saturday in August, consulting the small Liddell and Scott.

One of my chief objections to the management of the universe is that we suffer so much more from our gentler and more amiable vices than from our darkest crimes.

Letter to Grant Richards

Housman's cap, like a damp bun or pad of waste which engine-drivers clean their hands on.

A. C. Benson

DEAN INGE

The most successful religion is a superstition which has enslaved a philosophy.

Of all tyrannies a country can suffer, the worst is the tyranny of the majority.

Penury of personal character is the wasting disease of modern democracy.

Middle-aged people are often happier than the young: but it by no means follows that they ought to be.

Never put a man entirely in the wrong if you can help it.

The Revised Prayer Book: a sort of attempt to suppress burglary by legalizing petty larceny.

Prayer gives a man the opportunity of getting to know a gentleman he hardly ever meets. I do not mean his maker, but himself.

A. B. Ramsay: I think young men need to be reminded of that more than anything . . . .

W. R. I.: We all do.

> [*The discussion of a spiritual truth. A. B. Ramsay wrote,*
> *14 December 1948, 'I had forgotten this; but I do*
> *remember:*
> A.B.R.: *"Am I right in telling undergraduates to be*
> *ambitious?"*
> W.R.I.: *"Yes* – at their age.*"*]

Oh *dear*, – is there no Protestant worship left? (June 1938)

There are no Christian politics, and no Christian economics: only a Christian standard of values, and a Christian law of love.

It is useless for sheep to pass resolutions in favour of vegetarianism.
Of the League of Nations

Organized religion is a potent antiseptic. It prevents gains from being lost, and abuses from being removed. It is the last refuge of the savage in us, and it guards the sacred fire.

Asia will have a long deferred revenge on her arrogant younger sister.

There is no scripture against putting old wine into new bottles.

Hero-worship is pooled self-esteem.

Because most of the saints were poor, it does not follow that most of the poor are saints.

DR. JOHNSON AND BOSWELL

1. Johnson would not order Frank to fetch his favourite cat, as it was 'not good to employ human beings in the service of animals'.
2. Johnson said to the young officer sent by Sir Joseph Knight to accompany him to the shore from *Ramilies*, 'Sir, have the goodness to thank the Commodore . . . and tell Mr. —, the 1st

Lieutenant, that I beg he will leave off the practice of swearing.'
He replied that . . . His Majesty's service required it. 'Then
pray, Sir, tell Mr. — that I beseech him not to use one more oath
than is absolutely required for the service of His Majesty.'

3. Boswell told the King that he had difficulty in deciding what to
call the unfortunate grandson of James II whose adventures he
proposed to narrate. 'Why,' replied the King, 'call him the
unfortunate grandson of James II.'

4. To Miss B—, who thought of becoming a Catholic: 'Never
extend your beliefs, or you may turn Turk.'

Cornelia Knight, Autobiography *(1831)*

1. Johnson's voice low (i.e. gentle) and 'rather feminine': also high
(as opposed to bass).

2. Dinner was brought out to him and set on the ground: he would
be seen 'lying idly and cutting the grass with a knife' while
waiting.

Leigh Hunt, in The Indicator *(1834), vol. 2, p. 324, 'A*
Walk from Dulwich to Brockham'. Conversation with an old
man breaking stones 'at the end of the village', at Streatham

1. The turnpike roads had 'destroyed all refuges for elegant or
genteel poverty'.

2. No one in Ireland wears even the mask of incorruption.

Windham Papers

The most unaccountable part of Johnson's character was his total
ignorance of the character of his most familiar acquaintance.

Baretti, MS. note in Piozzi, Letters

Why, Sir, you should press yourself into the generality of mankind.

JOWETT

A woman can survive all partings but one: parting from her luggage.

The secret of influence is not sympathy . . . but a consistent life.

Be a reformer, but don't be found out.
> *Said to Warre. (A. B. Ramsay added: Most schoolmasters*
> *are reformers in order to be found out.)*

Never marry the only good one of a family.

A man cannot become young by over-exerting himself.

Sometimes – it is at least a harmless superstition – remembering you in prayer . . . .

The slight personification arising out of Greek genders is the greatest difficulty in translation.

We have sought truth, and sometimes perhaps found it. But have we had any *fun*?

I hope our young men won't become such *dodgers* as these old men are. I believe everything a young man says to me.

High Church principles can never be really impressed upon the poor.

It was very unfair to those young men . . . .
> *Of Newman's followers after his conversion*

No married clergyman should refuse a bishopric.

Families ought to be noisy. Far better than going to sleep.
> *To Lady Stanley of Alderley, 1866*

Do as everyone else does unless it is positively wrong.
A woman should never have the character of an *esprit fort*.
> *Amberley Papers*

Don't dispute about texts. Buy a good text.

A man is his own best adviser – if he's wise enough to ask for the advice.
> *To Boyd Carpenter*

Learn just enough of the subject to enable your mind to get rid of it.
Of metaphysics

If a man has studied himself out of religion, he must study himself into it again. (1852)

When a friend is attacked in mixed company, hang out a flag of opposition. (1885)

The way to get things done is not to mind who gets the credit of doing them.

Don't let that boy read too much. Let him read four books over and over again: *Arabian Nights*, *Pilgrim's Progress*, Plutarch's *Lives*, *Robinson Crusoe*.
To Mrs. Moss, of Claude Beaufort Moss

Nowhere probably is there more true feeling, and nowhere worse taste, than in a churchyard.

Young men make great mistakes in life. For one thing, they idealize love too much.

'Lord Albert Osborne, your gun will be returned to you when you go down or if you take your degree.' (No emphasis on 'when' or 'if'.)
Oral tradition, possibly deriving from W. P. Ker

A good writer, but too trustful. He sees a Bishop's son in a good living, and thinks it's a case of hereditary aptitude.
Of a writer on Eugenics

He was a remarkable man . . . and I never quite did him justice.
Funeral sermon on R. L. Nettleship: last sentence

Men get lazy, and substitute quantity of work for quality.

I have come to an age when it is best not to aim at a complete holiday.

I should like everyone to feel that these had been the best years of his life: though I shouldn't expect him to say it in the presence of his wife.

At a bump-supper

'It was Jowett who saved me from going to the dogs: or rather, brought me back when I had already gone there.'
It is like Morier to say that: it was kind of him: and it is quite true.

'Research' is a mere excuse for idleness.

It is important in this world, Costelloe, to be pushing – but it is fatal to seem so.

I had no idea that there was a perfectly sensible poet in the world.

Of Browning

Begin with the others, and do what the others do. Later you can branch off.

To E. P. Warren

No one who has a great deal of energy will long be popular in Oxford. (1882)

'Mr. Master, . . . '
'Don't be silly.'

There is a great deal of hard lying in the world: especially among people whose characters are above suspicion.

When you've educated the middle classes, Mr. Woodard, will they still be the middle classes?

> [*The Revd. Nathaniel Woodard (1811–91), educational reformer. Founded in 1848 the Woodard Society for the establishment of schools on public school lines and in accordance with the principles of the Oxford Movement. These schools were divided into three categories: for the Middle Class, the Middle Middle Class, and the Lower Middle Class.*]

To do much good, you must be a very able and patient man: and a bit of a rogue, too: and a good sort of roguery is, never to say a word against anyone, however well deserved.

Precautions are always blamed. When successful, they are said to be unnecessary.

To Dicey

Get called to the Bar: keep your eye on politics: translate Zeller's *History of Aristotelian Thought*.

To J. A. Symonds

The great thing in criticizing art is good *sense*. Goodbye.

To C. E. Montague, November 1886

We are not to *challenge* the world, Mr. Woodard.

R. A. KNOX

Balliol Chapel preserving a tradition of 'superior' music, indefinite dogma, and manly sentiment vaguely supposed to propitiate the *manes* of Jowett.

It's not the taste of water I object to. It's the after-effects.

As I don't drink alcohol, and giving up smoking would be far too serious a matter, I propose to stand in with Edward Lyttelton and give up Gibraltar: it's not such a habit with me.

The room smelt of not having been smoked in.

This question, unlike the platform at the railway station at which we have just arrived, has two sides to it.

At the Cambridge Union

Boys with perfectly brushed hair, coming into Chapel. I wondered what they would do in the land where partings are no more.

In Eton magazine

He did not make truth an idol, but he had almost a worship for candour.

Of P. H. Shaw-Stewart

I do not see ghosts: I only see their inherent probability.

He grew up from manhood into boyhood.

Of G. K. Chesterton

If the Magdalen had mistaken a gardener for Our Lord, that would have been hallucination . . . . No one can be so sure he has a half-crown in his pocket as the man who has mistaken it for a penny and looked again.

Safe remarks:
1. To inaudible remark: 'That's just what I've been wondering all the evening.'
2. 'I can never remember how you spell your name.' (But G. M. Young quoted the man who wearily replied, '*Still* J–O–N–E–S.')

When you become a Catholic you don't open your mouth and shut your eyes: just the opposite . . . .

DESMOND MacCARTHY

Real national characteristics:
1. English: an inflexible determination, in the face of truth, honour, and art, to have things both ways.
2. French: stinginess, and blind vindictive self-assertion.
3. Irish: readiness to spot stupidity, vulgarity, and pretentiousness: never to see through the passionate fool.

Drink . . . prevents you seeing yourself as others see you.

Samuel Butler's religion: a Broad Church paganism.

Disraeli: a flamingo in a farmyard.

Young people, not happy but resilient. The eupeptic chirpiness of middle age one of the most ridiculous mercies of life.

FALCONER MADAN

When dealing with any book before 1800, order up *all* the copies.

E. W. B. Nicholson [Bodley's Librarian] spending three days at the London Docks, watching outgoing ships, after losing a book from Bodley, which was afterwards discovered slightly out of place in the shelf.

G. M.

[*This section in the original notebooks is under assumed initials (H.L.C.). The reflections are nearly all Geoffrey Madan's own, except some quotations which he thought applied to himself.*]

King George, passing slowly in a closed car, looking like a big, rather worn *penny* in the window.

Every book is unique, and almost all books are rare. Few books are, or ever were, in perfect condition.

Small whisky and soda, a sort of Maundy money . . . .

An anthology for the forgotten sayings of great men, and the great sayings of forgotten men.

Never refuse a thing till you have the refusal of it.

Attractive Etonians who go straight on to the Stock Exchange missing the University on their fathers' advice: the raw material of the *great* bores.

To say you should treat a duke as an ordinary man is like telling you to read the Bible like an ordinary book.

A marquis is a sort of four-move chess-problem.

Warm lagoon of indolence and irreligion which seems to be the proper habitat of youth.

The great tragedy of the classical languages is to have been born twins.

The cat which isn't let out of the bag often becomes a skeleton in the cupboard.

There can be great selfishness hidden in generous hospitality.

G. M. Young – a pantomath.

Repington's *First World War* (1919) a shocking title.

> [*It presupposed another*]

Voice like water going out of a bath.
Face like the gate of a prison.

We need not be conscious of our faults, but we should not be unmindful of them.

Revd. E. Luce, precariously poised on the fringes of literacy and of gentility.

Laws are made to be broken, by law-abiding people.

Illiteracy, qualified by absenteeism.

> *Of Brooks's Club Library Committee*

Reasonable to ask young people to be adventurous, to go to the North Pole, say: but religion asks them to start off, without being sure if there *is* a North Pole.

It is dangerous to be right for the wrong reasons: but fatal to be wrong for the right ones.

Efficiency is not often the sister, and never the parent, of humour.

The odd fact that one sees Paddington as two such different places when arriving and when departing.

I love drink, so long as it isn't in moderation.

He talks as a man talks at lunch at an Embassy.

J. G., like a public meeting talking to *you*. Deciding an intricate question in the time, and the tone of voice, suitable to someone telling a man what to pack for a weekend visit.

G. H. : the face of a man killed in the South African war.

B. H. Sumner not so much a fine-looking man as a charcoal sketch of one.

Bussell, in B.N.C., alluding to the devil as 'Satanas', in tones of respectful familiarity.

There are people who should be careful to amortize the charm of their youth.

Compassion is human; sympathy, angelic; apathy, divine.

The last dream of bliss: staying in heaven without God there.

Even in the material side of his career, in his business life, there often seemed to be an undertone of the spiritual.
Of Lord Courtauld-Thomson

Importance of numbers in book-titles:
  Lives of Twelve *Good Men*
  Three *Weeks*
  Forty-one *Years in India*
  Ten Thousand *a Year*
  Twenty Thousand *Leagues under the Sea*
  A Tale of Two *Cities*

Sworded/sordid: an absurd homonym.
    [*Julian Grenfell's 'Orion's sworded hip' was often quoted
                                      with appreciation*]

Gladstone's Virgil quotations, like plovers' nests: impossible to see till you've been shown.

The only chance for genius is to have talent as well.

There are times when one can forgive a man almost anything if he has the inessential attributes of a gentleman.

To change an opinion without a mental process is the mark of the uneducated.

A l'heure où l'on enterrait Gounod, je suis allé voir l'automne à Versailles.

> [*Maurice Barrès*, Du sang, de la volupté, de la mort. *Quoted often by G.M. with amusement as an example of French morbidity*]

Treachery is of the very essence of snobbery.

Happiness, only a by-product.

Never advise people about their advisers.

The laws of Christianity: like the old speed-limit regulations . . . .

Snobbery, after all, is only a graduated conception of one's fellow-creatures.

It is hard to be a good king: but very hard to be a bad one. (1936)

Sese agebat [Virgil]: 'footing slow' [Milton].

Alive, in the sense that he can't legally be buried.

The Times obituary department: emotion anticipated in tranquillity.

Newcastle buildings, not coal-black but the colour of coke or slag.

He ought to take yes for an answer.

Letter addressed to 'Rooks' Club' delayed by going via House of Commons.

Different birds feeding: as if we had communal meals, and niggers 18 feet high suddenly appeared.

Peers: a kind of eye-shade or smoked glass, to protect us from the full glare of Royalty.

Finds, perhaps, in Charing Cross Road: bargains in Bond Street.

Montagu Norman (5 December 1941) at third-class guichet at Liverpool Street Station: like an old Rumanian Jew begging for alms.

Panshanger: day breaking hot and hard, like morning in the tropics: you find yourself sitting in tight to breakfast, in the full glare of talk, discussing immortality.

> [*Of a house-party at Lord and Lady Desborough's*]

Don's room, like the nest of a foolish bird.

I return your letter, which is one that I cannot possibly consent to receive: . . . I should urge your client to observe, and to ensure that his dog observes, the standards of behaviour proper to their respective levels of creation.

Hopeless munificence of Lord Nuffield.

The hateful blend of asceticism and humbug which hides under the hat of the teetotaller.

Conservative ideal of freedom and progress: everyone to have an unfettered opportunity of remaining exactly where they are.

The amount there is *of* it: the little there is *to* it.

> *Of Ardkinglas* [*a large sporting estate in Argyllshire acquired by Sir Andrew Noble, Marjorie Madan's grand-father*]

Michael Babington-Smith: like a boy who has not only won, but is in the act of receiving, a good-conduct prize at Charterhouse.

To discard magnificence, and remain magnificent, is the inimitable privilege of aristocracy.

JOHN MURRAY (1879–1964)

'Forward', on letters.

I saw criminal instability in his back: backs can be very expressive.

In the Greek language, there is a sort of tenderness towards that which has to be expressed.

NELSON

I make it a rule to introduce my midshipmen to all the good company I can. . . .

All we get is honour and salt beef.

Close with a Frenchman, but out-manoeuvre a Russian.

It matters not at all in what way I lay this poker on the floor. But if Bonaparte should say it *must* be placed in this direction, we must instantly insist upon its being laid in some other one.

DR. PARR

Commands admit many gradations of obedience.

He loved Hebrew, and he understood Greek.

Of Bishop Horne

He that acknowledges a God must at least admit the possibility of a miracle.

RICHARDSON

A kept mistress is the slave of a slave.

A prodigal man generally does more injustice than a covetous man.

Singularity in dress shews something wrong in the mind.

When grievances are to be enumerated, slight matters are often thrown in to make weight, that otherwise would not be complained of.

When a lover is easy, he is sure.

Love gratified is love satisfied, and love satisfied is indifference begun.

Old bachelors, when they like a woman, frequently think they have nothing to do but to persuade themselves to marry.

Meekness offended has an excellent memory, and can be bitter.

There is often more indelicacy in delicacy than very nice people are aware of.

Love is a narrower of the heart.

The woman who marries a man to get rid of his importunity, falls upon an *odd*, but perhaps *sure*, expedient.

In the wedded life, more obedience is sometimes practised by the party who vow'd it not, than by the party who did.

In the abusive sense of the word, there are old maids of twenty, and among widows and wives of all ages and complexions.

Some children act as if they thought their parents had nothing to do, but to see them established in the world, and then quit it.

QUEEN MARIE OF RUMANIA

When a man loves his children with an excess of passion, be sure that he is not happy.

Coquetry is not always an allurement: it is sometimes a shield.

A woman's virtue ought indeed to be great: since it often has to suffice for two.

Between husband and wife a shadow of courtship should always subsist.

LORD WELLESLEY

A very gentlemanly man. A very agreeable man – when he had his own way.

> *Duke of Wellington, to Count d'Orsay the day after Lord Wellesley's death. (But saying later that he had never thought any honour he had ever received equal to that of being Lord Wellesley's brother)*

Lord Normanby, in recklessly opening the Irish gaols, has exchanged the customary attributes of Mercy and Justice: he has made Mercy blind, and Justice weeping.

Little Charlie Gore, little Charlie Gore, remember what I tell you – my brother Arthur is the greatest ass that ever lived.

To Bishop Gore's father, in Dublin

H. G. WELLS

To Arnold Bennett: 'You paint like royalty.'

No knee-joint, but a sort of dispersed flexibility of leg.

A man's biography should be written by a conscientious enemy.

Muddle and waste caused by trained blockheads.

Who did the dressmaking for the ladies of the Merovingian Court? And how was it paid for ?

Popular writers on primitive man make out the early savage to be a sort of city clerk camping out. They present the men of early Egypt as the population of Paris or Chicago in fancy dress.

To see a novel proposition pass through a Marxist gathering is like watching a breeze across a field of ripe corn. It passes: and the serried minds return to their upstanding integrity.

I've put my mistress in cold storage for a bit.

At Reform Club, after his wife's death

ARCHBISHOP WHATELY
[Richard Whately (1787–1863), Archbishop of Dublin]

All men wish to have truth on their side: but few to be on the side of truth.

To disjoin the means of grace from the fruits of grace is to convert a sacrament into a charm.

Honesty is the best policy: but he who acts on that principle is not an honest man.

It is only given to the pure in heart to see the expediency of truth.

Virtue is goodness in a state of warfare (and therefore not applicable to God).

Pride is the best cure for vanity.

To learn a man's character, mark how he takes a favour.

Some speak and write as if they wanted to say something: others as if they had something to say.

Selfishness is very different from want of feeling.

Stingy people are not always selfish.

Selfishness is caught from those who have least of it.

Happiness is no laughing matter.

HUMBERT WOLFE

Of Arnold Bennett:
1. His little movement of the head, like a great pugilist just dodging his opponent's right.
2. Balancing his eyes over his mouth (like a conjuror).
3. He would look at his chosen prey with a fierce flat eye and the air of a man refusing to finance a tin-mine.

G. M. YOUNG

Four most efficient institutions in England: police, railways, trade unions, joint stock banks, founded 100 years ago by the same Conservative Government.

Aphorisms should be perfectly clear in form, but with receding distances of meaning.

No word for 'shallow' or 'chip' in French.

Lady Phipps receiving visits of condolence on Galsworthy's death.

Maîtresse dinante.
> *An amusing woman to whom you give a restaurant meal*

Lecky in his *Map of Life* says there is no petition one should proffer more earnestly than for a timely end. I should restate this by praying never to become a well-preserved old man.

The philosophy of Lucretius, as a subject, was like the religion of Milton: a sort of iron grid which kept the poem together.

Lord Parmoor: apparently made of bitter oil.

Birrell a sort of nonconformist Belloc.

Cabinet procedure: Asquith sat in middle of long side of table, and began by asking the Foreign Secretary to report. Peel went over the agenda with the departmental heads first.

Gladstone did nothing for the people: he wished for their prosperity only as a source of taxation.

Disraeli made Victoria feel useful.

Victorian nerves: why so good? By modern theories of repression, they ought all to have been raving lunatics. Yet Gladstone addressed the Cabinet for three hours, without interruption: and received the reply in Edinburgh, from a working-man, that sermons ought to be an hour long at least, because no passage of Scripture could possibly be expounded in less.

Mrs. Asquith belongs spiritually to the demi-monde: should have been the mistress of Foch, or the Kaiser.

Lord Beaverbrook looking like a doctor struck off the roll for performing an illegal operation.

A gentleman: superficially perhaps, a man who never looks as if he'd just had his hair cut.

Great prose may occur by accident: but not great poetry.

Treasury in 1850 kept a half-wit to make a nominal field against the official candidates. On one occasion he was successful.

'What are you doing this afternoon?'
'I don't know.'
'O yes, you do: you're having tea with me.'

> *Conversation of Canning and Lord Liverpool about*
> *1790: perhaps the first recorded 'undergraduate talk'*

Montagu Corry and Sir Philip Rose, bending close to Disraeli on his deathbed, *thought* that his last words were in Hebrew.

Three laws of sex:
1. No marriage without children.
2. No children without marriage.
3. *Ama et fac quod vis.*

Railway journey a perishable commodity: tickets should be auctioned at the last minute to avoid loss.

Montagu Norman's influence due to being a nervous man: the effect of a woman threatening to fly into a tantrum; men leave the room, as women do when men swear.

Members of Arthur's seem all to be men from good schools and bad colleges.

Christ never criticized by his equals. Good health-doctor. Saw that the ideal life was a well regulated *Fantasie-Leben*. Only really objected to pompousness, cruelty to children, and religious observance.

Objection to Ramsay Macdonald 'summoning' an actor to a box: to summon is a completed act, proper to Royalty.

Noise in Brooks's upstairs: moving the remains of the dead Duke.

French have more avenues for provincial ambition.

Asquith thought a job finished when he had decided the right course: Lloyd George when someone had run a bayonet into someone else.

Archives of Turkish Foreign Office kept in saddlebags. 'So much more convenient if you have to move quickly.'

Pedantry is greater accuracy than the case requires.

Steward at Arthur's having the gestures with which Lord John Russell would have shown Lord Palmerston to a seat at a private concert in Downing Street.

Can a nation exist with a strong artistic impulse and urge to grasp and externalize its impressions, but no sense of beauty?
Etruscans perhaps, or Germans?

Influenza symptoms seem only a slight intensification of one's ordinary attitudes to life: disinclination to get up, etc.

Women in the *aggregate*, unbearable.

Originals of metres in poetry:

George Darley ['Serenade of a Loyal Martyr']	Meredith, *Love in the Valley*
Johnson ['Long expected one and twenty']	Housman, *A Shropshire Lad* [passim]
J. H. Frere	Byron, *Don Juan*
Ben Jonson	Tennyson, *In Memoriam*

Rum, like an Icelander's vermouth.

A. E. Housman's epitaph: the only member of the middle classes who never called himself a gentleman.

Diplomatic career provides the consolations of old age in middle life.

Some good moralist (? Newman) held that falsehood was defensible, in the face of an attempt to extract personal information by direct question.

'It is the cause': theory that Othello closes and lays down a *Bible*.

Christ in A.D. 35 thought of rather like Lord Knutsford.
> [*Sidney Holland, 2nd Viscount Knutsford (1855–1931),*
> *philanthropist, Chairman of the London Hospital,*
> *and an exceptionally successful fund-raiser*]

Use of words 'vision' and 'supremely' an infallible sign of the uneducated.

Dignum laude virum Musa vetat mori.
> *Horace, Odes, IV. viii: Antonius Musa was Court Physician*

The aesthetic movement in England started by Mr. Gladstone.
> *Article on Ritualism*

Irwin was sent to India to see that the Indians were given enough rope: Willingdon, to make sure they hanged themselves.

To accent Greek, as absurd as writing it on papyrus.

Little left of religion in Ruskin by 1879 except an adolescent horror of fornication.

At the Methodist Union celebration King George, following an irreproachable precedent, sent his son to represent him.

How many l's in 'lily': an instance of a 'mental reservation', in casuistry.

The danger of having an educated king is that he would be bound to find some section of his subjects ridiculous.

Fixed prices in retail trade started by Quakers about 1840, who saw profits in children being able to shop for parents.

Notice in Tashkent: 'forbidden to *day-dream*'.

A Colonel describing the Chinese Exhibition: 'The attendants were all Gunners.' Shakespearian quality of this comment.

1. Every subject of the Crown is entitled to make pickles.
2. Every man must bear the name of his father.
Sir John Markham, Chief Justice, 1465

Middle-aged people, like middle-class people, hate those on each side of them.

Asquith, typical of the disintegration towards 1890: a lost soul, as soon as he became a Soul.

Cyril Asquith, entering Brooks's: like a young Yorkshire miner coming back to the cottage (15 December 1936).

Be gentle, as you fold away a cast-off creed.

Christ, with a healthy, well-to-do country upbringing, taking adultery lightly. What got him into trouble was answering fools according to their folly.

Lawn-tennis, originally known as Sphairistike.

Paddington, 'seen so differently according as one arrives or departs': perhaps the difference between life seen in youth and old age.
[*Cf. p. 67*]

Stanley Baldwin's second sight: realizing that his great task was to educate the Labour Party: result, no one lost a night's sleep when they came in.

When a man is a bit of a woman, one does like that bit to be a lady.
On Horace Walpole, Sunday Times, *5 December 1937*

Wordsworth colour-blind: saw sand the same colour as grass.

Conservative: a man with an inborn conviction that he is right, without being able to prove it.
Revd. T. James, 1844

Children: unable to understand the concept of uncertainty.

Winston Churchill in conversation, like an old ironclad, not easy to turn or manoeuvre: not answering the helm.

Is he alive, d'you know? When last heard of, he was alive.

Let me counsel my friends of the working-classes not to raise their eyes too far: or too fast.

Gladstone

The fascination, to a crowd, of anything going up the side of a building on a rope or lift: exceedingly primitive.

Dicey lecturing to one grocer in All Souls, in a snowstorm.

To forget your own good sayings is the mark of intellectual aristocracy.

Hitler, Lloyd George, Jesus Christ: Messianic types, not liars.

Somewhere in *D.N.B*: the lost Scottish community, long unable to read or write: preserving one relic only of Protestantism, that *if* they got hold of any meat, they kept it till Friday to eat.

Duke of Windsor (October 1939). A gentleman; a major in a not quite first-class regiment, and not likely to go further than that; happily married to a devoted wife, not his equal but doing her best to live up to him.

VII

VINIANA

1. Sherry gives rise to no *thoughts*.
2. Body . . . means that the wine holds in solution a large quantity of matter capable of being tested by the nerves of taste.

R. Druitt (1865)

They don't know how good it is for them.

Master of Trinity to me, after complaining that under-graduates no longer drank port

I have been advised, at my age, not to attempt to give up alcohol.

Bishop H. (Christmas message to British Expeditionary Force, 1915)

Port: the milk of donhood.

Max Beerbohm

All port tastes the same after lunch.

C. M. Wells

There is something in port which is in pre-established harmony with the best English character.

Saintsbury

'Only half-full, thank you.' Shy woman, with Savoy brandy-glass.

Pouring overheated wine from cold glass to cold glass (commended by C. M. Wells).

Berry thinking 1923 was 1907, and *not minding*: 'Odd how it's come on.'

Amyas Warre putting tiny piece of ice into a glass of port, at a dinner in his honour.

> [*Often quoted by G.M.: the expert was not afraid to do
> what an amateur would have thought wrong*]

Je ne fais pas chambrer les vins de Bourgogne.

> *MS. note in wine-list at Lion d'Or, Bayeux (1938)*

We drank champagne out of a saucer of ground glass mounted on a pedestal of cut glass.

> *Disraeli to his sister, 1832* [*Champagne glasses were an
> innovation*]

He had been very ill . . . . He looked old and frail, and was unusually silent; but over the second glass of port – the doctors were building him up – he began to mend.

> *R. W. Chapman, of Ingram Bywater*

Queen Victoria 'strengthening' claret with whisky.

> *Gladstone, letter to Mrs. Gladstone, 1864*

Monk, aged 96, at Eitelsbach: dying of *ullage* when daily allowance was cut down to one litre.

'Will you drink more port, Mr. Dean?'
'When I have finished that which is before me.'

> *Mr. Gladstone's favourite story of Dean Waddington*

Mouse, after drinking a drop of Monbazillac: 'Now where is that bloody cat?'

I see you have been brought up in the best school, – the school of port: and if you will take an old man's advice, Sir, always drink it out of a claret-glass.

> *The Revd. F. Bertie, to Lord Ernle at All Souls*

The Revd. Mr. Wilkins (1847) to Sidgwick: 'Don't get drunk before dinner: you can't really enjoy it.'

Three pieces of earnest advice from the Revd. H. J. Bidder, aged 86, after sitting silent, with a crumpled face, all through dinner, and once loudly asking the man opposite who I was:

1. Never drink claret in an East wind.
2. Take your pleasures singly, one by one.
3. Never sit on a hard chair after drinking port.

VIII

DE PECUNIA

Sir Abe Bailey with four relations, but only £3,000,000: dying under the impression that there must be something wrong with arithmetic.

Man like a scarecrow, at country auction bidding £50,000 for a property: deposit asked for : refused: one banknote given: referred to Bank of England: perfectly genuine: one of three in existence.

F. W. Winterbotham [once solicitor to the Madan family]

Lord Cunliffe, giving evidence before a Royal Commission, at the special request of the Chancellor of the Exchequer, would only say that the Bank of England reserves were 'very, very considerable'. When pressed to give an even approximate figure, he replied that he would be 'very, very reluctant to add to what he had said'.

Harrison Hayter (1825–98) [G.M.'s maternal grandfather], President of the Institute of Civil Engineers, holding nothing but Consols and Corporation Stocks: not seaside corporations, however, as light-minded people tend to go to the seaside, and also the South Coast might be attacked by the French.

O. T. Falk's father, if a share he had bought went up, writing to the transferor to offer a refund.

It depends on the rupee-value of the dollar in three months' time. . .

J. M. Keynes (quoted by Cyril Asquith)

1. You don't make money by speculation. You make money by buying good shares, and keeping them.
2. Never be ashamed of going small.

Sir George Jessel

Never hesitate to give top prices for what you want.

T . J. Wise

Don't argue with the tape.
Don't buck the market.

American sayings

Put all your eggs in one basket: and watch that basket.

Andrew Carnegie

James Morrison, of Basildon Park: fortune made in three ways, crape, gloves, and standing instructions to his broker to buy and sell Consols within limits of 99⅛–⅜: afraid of dying poor: losing nine million pounds.

IX

ANECDOTES

Lunch party given by Lady Colefax 'To meet the Mother of the Unknown Warrior'.

Pius IX to the Bishop of Gibraltar: 'Then I am in your Diocese.'

'Good. Now there'll be more room in the car.'
H. W. B. Joseph: 'Well, no, surely: not more room, only less of it occupied.'

U.S. child saying prayers: praying for *God*: 'If anything happens to him, we're properly sunk.'

Mr. Justice Darling to F. E. Smith: 'Always interesting to watch the impact of two minds, both fresh to the case.'

Now I know the meaning of the word grotesque.
Sydney Smith, on Mrs. Grote's turban

Treasury minute, on War Office confusion of Clothing and Victualling Department: 'Clothes are no doubt an essential provision, but they can only in extreme emergency be classified as victuals.'

Philip Guedalla at Cambridge Union, 1913: 'The mysterious grain-elevating building, close to the station, which I always think of as Balliol College, Cambridge.'

Margot: You're *fond* of me, and of Etty, and Blanchie: but you don't really care – you wouldn't *mind* if we all died.
Balfour: I should mind if you all died on the same day.

Moltke, only laughing twice in his life . . . .
> [*Once when his mother-in-law died, and once when a
> certain fortress was declared to be impregnable*]

D. A. Winstanley: 'Gow has an inferiority complex about other people.'

Mrs. Cornish: 'One day he will surprise us all.'
> [*Said encouragingly of a small rather unpromising Eton boy*]

Hier gibt es kein gemütliches Familienleben.
> *German lecturer on the Palatine* [*to German woman
> tourist who kept asking for the rooms of the Empress*]

I like the poor, the respectful poor.
> *F. W. Bussell*

A. C. Ainger disliking long journeys and spending night at Ealing.

And now let's talk about Northumberland.
> *Sir Edward Grey to Sir John Noble (2 August 1914)*

Welsh sermon: the word 'truth' heard repeatedly uttered in English: apparently 'no exact equivalent' in Welsh.

Young man at smart house: only a black tie brought: asking advice from an older fellow-guest: 'My dear fellow, fire your man.'

Two psychiatrists meeting: 'You're pretty well, how am I?'

Lord French at Maubeuge, recalling Hamley's comment on Bazaine at Metz: ' . . . the anxiety of the temporizing mind which prefers postponement of a crisis to vigorous enterprise: in clinging to Metz he acted like one who, when the ship is foundering, should lay hold of the anchor.'
> [*In consequence Lord French's tactics were successful*]

Lord Goschen (1886): 'We will make our wills and do our duty.'
> [*Irish crisis: response, after a threat of assassination, when it was
> pointed out that his party would be embarking on a Friday*]

Hornby in 1837, confusion in praying for the new Queen: 'King of Queens, Lord of Ladies, and only Ruler of Princesses.'

Moses Griffith, when Dr. Wootten said his maxim was 'Eat and leave off hungry': 'Why not wash and leave off dirty?'

Dr. Frowd: reading lessons: becoming husky when denouncing the wicked: drawing out a lozenge: reading the marginal variants half out loud, and shaking his head or nodding and smiling.

Pater to Bussell, not staying to watch hockey match where A. L. Smith and other dons were playing: 'I don't think it's quite fair.'

Russian third-degree interrogator to Keeling: 'How do you manage to look so fit and well, after being woken up in the middle of the night, and asked these endless questions . . . ?'
'Oh that's all right: I've been married sixteen years.'

I hope so: I believe so: I always say so.
        Pater, when asked if he was related to the French painter Pater

American girl on the Commandments: 'They don't tell you what you ought to do: and they only put ideas into your head.'
        Elizabeth Bibesco

'Why do you go and hear Spurgeon when you don't believe a word he says?'
'Ah, but *he* does.'
        James Martineau

Boy, wanting to be a 'retired business man'.

A very old negro said, if he could get through March, he usually found he lived till the end of the year.

I never had any contemporaries.
        Lord Acton

Conscience-money of 17 years dog-licence sent to Kingsley Wood [Chancellor of the Exchequer].

They say I am against reform; I am not against reform. There is a time for everything, and the time for reform is when it can no longer be resisted.

Duke of Cambridge

Mysterious frame, with ivory measuring-strip, in sub-basement of 148 Piccadilly [the Rothschilds' London house]. For measuring footmen: if one grew too fast, he could be exchanged for one from Tring.

Talleyrand, dining with the Duke of Wellington, when Napoleon's death was announced: 'Ce n'est pas un événement, c'est une nouvelle.'

Disraeli, of an air-cushion: 'Take away that emblem of mortality.' (1880)

Lady on a hot day in Cairo: 'Ninety-two this morning, Colonel Lawrence! Ninety-two. What do you say to that?'
T. E. Lawrence: 'Many happy returns of the day.'

'Oh, Mr. Spurgeon, that was wonderful.'
'Yes, Madam; so the Devil whispered into my ear as I came down the steps of the pulpit.'

Lord Cowley on Napoleon III: 'Il ne parle jamais, et il ment toujours.'

Dr. Perkins (1870) in the gutter: 'Save the others: I can swim.'

Dr. Bertie, engaging prize-fighter as servant, in case Roman Catholic priest should contrive entrance during a seizure and procure his reception into the heretical Church.

Bishop X: 'Ah, Ma'am, we cannot pray too often or too fervently for the Royal Family.'
Queen Victoria: 'Not too fervently, no: but too often, yes.'

Sir J. S. did not mind people looking at their watch during his address, only minded their holding it up to their ear.

Arnold Bennett sending F.F.'s writing to a graphologist: reply beginning, 'Cette vieille femme acharnée . . . .'

[*Of F. F. Madan, G.M.'s brother*]

Lady Desborough c. 1879 at Wrest: seeing Lady Rothschild ask Lady Salisbury where she got her hats: no answer: asking again: 'Oh, I don't know': poking up the corner of her hat to look.

Mr. and Mrs. Thomas Hardy:
'You haven't had any fresh air, or spoken to a single soul for twelve days.'
'Yes I have. I opened the window, and spoke to the man who drives the manure-cart.'
'What did you say?'
'"Good morning."'

Lady Desborough's notebook

'Sir, you are in a devilish awkward predicament, and must get out of it as best you can.'

Duke of Wellington, when asked for advice

Zaharoff travelling always with two cooks: one to study *new* dishes.

Non-intervention is a metaphysical idea, indistinguishable in practice from intervention.

Talleyrand

'Precedent compels me to ask: what is jazz?'

Lord Hewart

'Why aren't you doing your bit to preserve the civilization we're fighting for?'
H. W. Garrod (1917): 'Madam, I *am* that civilization.'

I am fully convinced that the highest life can only be lived on a foundation of Christian belief: – or some substitute for it.

Henry Sidgwick to Arthur Sidgwick

New squire to preacher: 'Not at all, not at all: it would be a pretty poor sermon that didn't hit me somewhere.'

I am never intentionally obscure: – but I do not mean my poems to be taken as a substitute for a pipe.

Browning

President Routh (1755–1854):
1. To Pusey (1849): the 'late troubles': discovered to refer to the revolution of 1688.
2. Putting up a duplicate tablet in Theale Church, in case the brass of the first was melted down for a war.

Pio Nono to English visitor: 'How long have you been in Rome?'
'A month.'
'Ah, then you know *all* about it.'

Mysterious letters 'W.H.M.' after candidates for promotion on Lambeth list.

['*Wife has means': early 19th-century story*]

Monday at 3: such an *obscure* hour.
Mrs. Cornish: comment on plan for French reading
(C. H. K. Marten, Eton 1939)

Horse in the Row, shying at Mrs. Yates Thompson's carriage (1939).

[*It was only accustomed to motors*]

'Brothers of God', altered to 'children of God' by the Revd. B. W. Harvey, if Miss Goodford was in chapel.

Sir John Simon, supposed in a *Times* article to be 78 instead of 77, describing it as a 'wounding error'.

Well, anyhow I haven't made a graven image.
Country squire, after Mattins

'Right! First trick to you! Have a cigar.'

Bottomley to Plender
[*Horatio Bottomley (1860–1933), journalist, M.P.,
and fraudulent company promoter; William Plender
(1861–1946), created Baron Plender 1931, eminent
chartered accountant. Plender was presumably at some
point employed to examine Bottomley's affairs*]

Mahaffy, asked by a young man in a Dublin street if he was saved,
paused and answered: 'I am, but between you and me, it was a
damned close squeak.'

X

RECOLLECTIONS AND THINGS SEEN

We never had printed books here.

> *Mrs. Yates Thompson, 10 June 1932*
> *[They had a famous collection of MSS.]*

Two memories of Pater:
1. Discussing travel, he spoke of going 'north of the Humber', as if going far beyond civilization.
2. After his death, about 300 slips of paper were found, each with some word and an appropriate adjective written on it, which he meant to use in a book later on.

And one of F. W. Bussell:
  He would leave some curious object, like an old sword, on a table when a guest was coming, and watch the effect on the guest from a concealed place for a few moments before appearing.

> *A. J. Butler to me, in B.N.C., 1913*

Henry Yates Thompson:
1. 'I was at Gettysburg in 1863.'
2. At Harrow: cheering Lord Palmerston (1855) who had ridden down from London, and Baldwin (1925).

Tell them to play up.

> *Sir Herbert Lawrence, British Chairman of a foreign bank,*
> *when some slightly doubtful business proposal was made*

Robert Bridges saying of 'Abt Vogler': 'With one hand slap my thigh, with one pat God.'

It's not so easily disproved as that.

> *Arnold Bennett, in answer to G.M.'s remark when they were watching the Boat Race from A. P. Herbert's house and saw the great crowds on the opposite bank: 'Look at the numbers, that surely of itself would disprove the idea of survival after death.'*

Always remember, this is a thing that *can* be done very well.

> *Mrs. Alfred Lyttelton, 1919 [before opening a bazaar]*

George Rylands on Abyssinian hoax [when Bloomsbury intellectuals impersonated Abyssinian potentates at a Royal Navy review]: two middies heard saying, 'You haven't been in the East – they've the real nigger smell.'

Reminiscences of William Cory, told me by Father Williamson, when I was staying with Lord Esher, July 1928:

1. φίλον εἴη φιλεῖν: a favourite motto, on his ring.
2. The *nobility* of a cow walking towards you in a field.
3. Starting off with mixed party of boys, throwing top hat into field as a sign of festivity: returning at 3 a.m.
4. Lived at 2, High Street, Eton. Luxmoore told me 6, many times. The streets may have been renumbered, or he may have lived at both. But Luxmoore was very inaccurate.
5. Took parties to see pictures. 'Now tell me what *you* think beautiful.'
6. Boys used to throw soap at him from an upper floor as he sat in his bath.

Visit to J. Meade Falkner:

1. Last visit of Charles I to Durham: a cope especially made (and still existing), with David represented carrying Goliath's head.
2. A 'canon' of recumbent effigies: that they slope downwards from the breast; no paunch, like a dead dog floating on a canal.
3. W. S. Landor thought the three most romantic places in the world were Oxford, Durham, and Rome; *in that order*.

Talk with C. M. Wells in Norway (5 June 1934):

1. We Graces ain't no water-spaniels.
> [*W. G. Grace, refusing a bath after a cricket match*]
2. *Once* tired, at Sidmouth in 1892.

Visit to Max Beerbohm at Rapallo (21 January 1929):

1. Swinburne at The Pines had a 'continuous temple and cheek-bone': talked ecstatically of Tenniel's cartoons.
2. A. E. Housman like an absconding cashier? We certainly wished he would abscond. Sitting silent, then saying only, 'There's a bit of a nip in the air tonight, don't you think?'
3. King Edward's dinner to celebrate publication of the *D.N.B.* Leslie Stephen struck out: Canon Ainger included, after a troubled pause, as being an authority on *Lamb*.
4. Baron Corvo's eyes like oysters magnified: bad oysters magnified.

The Coin Speaks

Singers sing for coin: but I,
Struck in Rome's last agony,
Shut the lips of Melody.

Many years my thin white face
Peered in every market-place
At the Doomed Imperial Race.

Warmed against and worn between
Hearts uncleansed and hands unclean,
What is there I have not seen?

Not an Empire dazed and old,
Smitten blind and stricken cold,
Bartering her sons for gold;

Not the Plebs her rulers please
From the public treasuries
With the bread and circuses;

Not the hard-won fields restored,
At the egregious Senate's word,
To the savage and the sword;

Not the People's Godlike voice
As it welcomes or destroys
Month-old idols of its choice;

Not the legions they disband,
Not the oarless ships unmanned,
Not the ruin of the land,
These I know and understand.

[*Kipling wrote this poem on the fly-leaf of Sir Charles Oman's copy of* Puck of Pook's Hill, *and dated it 'June 1907'. Oman, the historian, was also a distinguished numismatist*]

A Short View of Mussolini

As I walked through the huge, hot 'lounge' of the Grand Hotel, on my way to dinner, I noticed a vague stir at the far end, and a group forming by the inner door: a few people in evening clothes, some young women, an old man with medals – a formal gathering of some kind. I waited. A man with a dark beard approached, highly villainous in aspect, like a captured Sicilian bandit (it was Volpi, the Finance Minister), and immediately behind him the Duce . . . . He held himself with an exaggerated stiffness, like a keen recruit at attention. His dress was not 'soigné', with crumpled trousers and heavy shoes. He was thick, pale, bald, fierce. Some rather theatrical orders hung from his coat, stars, chains or bright buttons, and from the pocket of his trousers there dribbled a great magenta scarf, the insignia of something else. He was alert and nervous. I noticed that he would glance suddenly round, and he caught my eye, twenty yards off, three or four times. Then he recovered himself and looked every inch a Dictator. This is of course exactly what a born ruler never does. King George would have been entirely oblivious of his surroundings, while Asquith would have mistaken the occasion and worn grey flannel trousers. Mussolini carefully occupied the middle of the stage, and as new-comers arrived he reassumed his position in the centre. He vanished into dinner (it was in honour of Titulescu). I was told there were twenty-five detectives concealed in the hotel for the evening . . . .

26 January 1928

Omne Magnificum pro Ignoto

This morning I saw a remarkable sight. I came up to the City in the Underground rather late, about half-past ten. At Bond Street a man got in whom I just know, and have spoken to three or four times in my life. He wore loose clothes, a ringed and jewelled tie, a crumpled black hat. His general presence made a most distinguished effect, suggesting all manner of romantic things: a Restoration poet, a historic French admiral, a bearded nobleman of Spain – the ideal which everyone would like to think his own great-grandfather attained, to adapt a famous obituary phrase. This strange being was in a state of high tension. He lay back looking half strangled, as if fallen from a great height, or praying to be supported in some heavy trial; darted a glance away, focussing a distant passenger and slowly dropping his chin; glared round with the queer look of a man swelling with laughter and longing to share it with someone else; or groaned aloud in pain. The carriage was half-full. A woman rose to get out at a station. He started and stared in horror, lifting both hands with delicate fingers, and crooning a song as if to calm a child. Then he fell back, with forehead deeply lined, a flicker of splendid hands, and a magnificent eye very wide open. Two or three people recognized the Governor of the Bank. In the inestimable English tradition they smiled faintly, assumed all to be somehow for the best, and let it go at that.

The train scraped round the rails at the Bank station, and emptied itself. Last but one, out of the last carriage, strolled this enigmatic figure. He struck out now in some odd rhythm, half-jaunty, half-defiant; bent idly down to peer all round an empty carriage; then slid past a group of people at a double pace: only to halt for a leisurely and mournful study of an advertisement on a wall. At the end he paused again, gazing nobly into the distance, like some fine old Swiss guide watching the signs of a storm. Soon he strode on and mounted the escalator, alone, like the bridge of a ship, striking a glorious pose – portrait of an admiral in China seas:

> Even in the presence of an enemy fleet,
> Between the steep cliff and the coming wave.

I thought of the Treasury saying, that the Bank of England acts like a commander in the days before strategy was thought of.

He had no ticket at the bar; and the same instinct which would not stare in the train, would not ask a question as he left the platform. As well demand a passport from a Czar. But the ticket was found at last, by its imperial owner, stuck in the band of his soft dark hat. Still the drama continued; a chuckle, a tormented backward glance, a sudden scrutiny of forbidden entrances. At the top, one last proprietary gaze at the vulgar novelties which press on the old symbolic temple of Threadneedle Street. The traffic was in full flow: it was instantly reined back as he approached: three men saluted. But the mysterious grandee had already slipped and sauntered out of sight, chin in air.

March 1932

XI

LIVRES SANS NOM

1929

La vérité est dans une nuance.
Renan

1. Si tu désires faire une chose, prends l'avis de tes amis: si tu veux la faire, ne consulte personne.

Princesse Karadja

2. Ce qu'il faut chercher: réalités ayant la magie du rêve.

Jean Dolent

3. J'ai changé bien des fois de certitude.

Jean Dolent

4. Si j'avais été la colombe, je ne serais pas rentrée dans l'Arche.
Mme Ackermann

5. Pour notre doctrine souhaitons le succès, jamais le triomphe.
Lucien Arréat

6. Ce n'est qu'en cherchant les mots qu'on trouve les pensées.
Joubert

7. L'art de savoir mettre en oeuvre de médiocres qualités donne souvent plus de réputation que le véritable mérite.

Abbé de la Roche

8. Quelque éclatante que soit une action, elle ne doit pas passer pour grande lorsqu'elle n'est pas l'effet d'un grand dessein.

Balzac

9. Il ne faut rien faire que de raisonnable, mais il faut bien se garder de faire toutes les choses qui le sont.

Montesquieu

10. De tous les sentiments, le plus difficile à feindre c'est la fierté.

Duc de Lévis

11. Ce ne sont pas toujours les fautes que nous perdent, c'est la manière de se conduire après les avoir faites.

Marquise de Lambert

12. Il y a de certains temps où de certaines gens ont toujours raison.

Cardinal de Retz

13. Le déluge n'a pas réussi: il est resté un homme.

Becque

14. Le vice a ses hypocrites comme la vertu.

Eugène Marbeau

15. Le malheur fait dans certaines âmes un vaste désert où retentit la voix de Dieu.

Balzac

16. Le moyen d'être cru est de rendre la vérité incroyable.

Anatole France

17. Les mots pompeux ne sont souvent que l'hommage que les illettrés rendent au dieu inconnu, le style.

M. Heyguet

18. Les qualités militaires ne sont pas toujours nécessaires.

Napoléon

19. Le caprice est la limaille du désir.

Commerson

20. Il y a une infection de goût qui n'est pas compatible avec la droiture de l'âme.

Sainte-Beuve

21. Une des plus grandes preuves de médiocrité, c'est de ne pas savoir reconnaître la supériorité là où elle se trouve.

Jean-Baptiste Say

22. Vauvenargues a dit vrai que les grandes pensées viennent du coeur, mais c'est l'esprit qui va les y chercher.

Vicomte d'Yzarn-Freissinet

23. Ne vous faites jamais des ennemis, et surtout des ennemis timides.

G. de Palajos

24. Dieu reconnaîtra ses anges par l'inflexion de leurs voix, et le mystère de leurs regrets.

Balzac

25. Je n'aime que les gens qui recèlent de l'infini.

Rémy de Gourmont

26. Le vraisembable est le plus grand ennemi qu'ait la vérité.

Abbé Serge

27. Faire aisément ce qui est difficile aux autres, voilà le talent: faire ce qui est impossible au talent, voilà le génie.

Henri Frédéric Amiel

28. Je demande qu'on interdise aux menteurs de dire la vérité.

Comte d'Houdetot

29. Les vocations manquées déteignent sur toute l'existence.

Balzac

30. Rien ne persuade tant les gens qui ont peu de sens que ce qu'ils n'entendent pas.

Cardinal de Retz

31. C'est le passé, l'obscur passé, qui détermine nos passions.

Anatole France

32. La mort semble née à Rome.

Chateaubriand

33. La seule chose qui a gâté pour moi la campagne de Russie, c'est de l'avoir faite avec des gens qui auraient rapetissé le Colisée ou la baie de Naples.

Stendhal

34. Rien ne marque tant le jugement solide d'un homme que de savoir choisir entre les grands inconvénients.

Cardinal de Retz

35. Combien de secrets sont trahis par vanité: on veut montrer qu'on était digne d'une confidence.

M. Stern

36. Aujourd'hui les nations ont leurs flatteurs comme jadis les rois.

Louis Philippe

37. Si la prose n'existait point, il ne faudrait pas l'inventer.

Balzac

38. C'est un grand signe de médiocrité de louer toujours modérément.

Vauvenargues

39. Il y a des conjonctures dans lesquelles on ne peut plus faire que des fautes: mais personne n'y tombe que ceux qui s'y précipitent.

Cardinal de Retz

('Excellent maxim but more suited to the meridian of France or Spain than of England.' *Lord Chesterfield*)

40. Décrire est déchoir de la majesté d'écrire.

Aurel

41. Le courage qu'on a eu fait souvent la meilleure partie de celui qu'on a.

A. Sogmonov

42. On a souvent un peu les qualités qu'on admire: et presque toujours celles qu'on déteste.

Abbé de Montfichet

43. Les hommes qui pensent toujours ce qu'ils disent ont le tort de se croire en droit de dire toujours ce qu'ils pensent.

Charles Lemesle

44. Fais que je me contredise souvent: afin d'être simple et vrai.

Prière païenne

45. Sache sourire quelquefois comme tu mets des fleurs sur une tombe.

A. Chauvilliers

46. La peur aime l'idée du danger.

Joubert

47. Il y a deux sortes d'ingratitude: l'une qui consiste à ne point reconnaître les services qu'on nous a rendus; l'autre, à n'en point accepter de ceux à qui nous avons eu le bonheur d'en rendre.

André de Prémontval

48. Personne d'un grand caractère ne craint d'avoir l'air d'être mené.

Mme de Genlis

49. On est souvent plus attaché à une certaine manière de vie qu'à la vie.

Sénac de Meilhan

50. Si les sots ne sont pas modestes, ce n'est pas leur faute; ils n'ont pas de quoi l'être.

J. Sanial Dubay

51. Toutes les misères de l'homme, ce sont misères de grand seigneur, misères d'un roi dépossédé.

Pascal

52. Il faut respecter le type que Dieu cherche à produire en nous.

Abbé Loisy

1930

Piis Manibus A.C.B.

1. On one day in the week, if possible, neither read nor write poetry.

   Chinese Rule of Health

2. No gentleman can be without three copies of a book; one for show (and this he will probably keep at his country house), another for use, and a third at the service of his friends

   Richard Heber

3. Cheerfulness is the daughter of employment: I have known a man return in high spirits from a funeral merely because he had had the management of it.

   Bishop Horne

4. Nobody blames Lucifer for not seeing the comic side of his fall.

   Bernard Shaw

5. Reckon right, and February hath 31 days.

   George Herbert

6. What we should pursue is the most convenient arrangement of our ideas.

   Samuel Butler

7. Though the dews of Divine Grace fall everywhere, yet they lie longest in the shade.

   Bishop Patrick

8. Churchgoers, and 'good' people generally, do just what ordinary decent people do about anything: only they do it slower.

   A. C. Benson

9. A rush of thoughts is the only conceivable prosperity that can come to us.

   Emerson

10. In this country it isn't a question of how much you can do: it's a question of how much you can stand.

    Lord Lyons (Ambassador to U.S.A.)

11. You must compute what you give for money.

    Dr. Johnson

12. The only palliative for vulgarity is uniform good-nature.

    Richard Duppa

13. Never drudge.
    Be precise, but not pedantic.

    Jowett

14. The transcendent capacity of taking trouble is the hall-mark of talent, never the seal of genius.

    Henry Ward

15. Those who cannot miss an opportunity of bringing in some opinion of their own are not to be trusted with the management of any great question.

    Hazlitt

16. The shadow of lost knowledge at least protects you from many illusions.

    William Cory

17. Man should not dispute or assert, but whisper results to his neighbour.

    Keats

18. a. The Three Follies:
    1. Coveting another's wife.
    2. Having no wife.
    3. Conferring power on a wife.

    b. The Three Faults:
    1. Unpleasant conduct.
    2. Impatience with old people.
    3. Want of faith in religious books.

c. The Three Illusions:
  1. To think investments secure.
  2. To imagine that the rich regard you as their equal.
  3. To suppose your virtues common to all, and your vices
     peculiar to yourself.

Chinese Litany

19. It is not for Christians to be like unto thistles or teazles, which a
man cannot touch without pricking his fingers; but rather to
pilosella, or mouse-ear, in our herbal, which is soft and silken in
the handling.

Bishop Hall

20. In Society, nothing must be discussed; give only results. In
Society, never think; always be on the watch.

Disraeli

21. Half-knowledge is very communicable; not so knowledge.

Mary Coleridge

22. He ought to be very well mounted who is for leaping the hedge
of custom.

Revd. Adam Hill

23. I should like to be an English peer until I reached 35. I would
then be a Marshal of France until 50, and afterwards go to
Rome, be a Cardinal and never die.

*Young officer of the French Navy, quoted in Cornelia
Knight's Memoirs (1831)*

24. No restraint is more irksome to a man than to be left to his own
discretion.

Archbishop Whately

25. Reasonable human conduct is part of the ordinary course of
things.

Lord Haldane (in a considered judgment)

26. It is almost too broadly comic that a necessity of life like water should be pumped to us from nobody knows where, by nobody knows whom, sometimes nearly a hundred miles away. It is every bit as comic as if air were pumped to us from miles away, and we all went about like divers at the bottom of the sea.

G. K. Chesterton

27. No arguments and no reproaches are more entirely on the side of error, or of more tendency to strengthen evil, than those set up against things truly good, only on the ground of the abuse of them.

Revd. John Miller (Sermon preached at Park Chapel, 1843)

28. There is only one line to be adopted in opposition to all tricks: that is the steady straight line of duty, tempered by forbearance, levity, and good nature.

Duke of Wellington

29. Work shapes the mind: leisure colours it.

Revd. James Dolbear (1861)

30. Always polish your sentences, and never use a verb in the passive.

Foch

31. Even in the circles of Hell there is the heroism of sinners who cling to each other in the fiery whirlwind and never recriminate.

George Eliot

32. Merely say, Prince Albert called.

The Prince Consort at Farringford, finding Tennyson out

33. S. Basil says, he saw an Oxe weepe for the death of his yoke-fellow: but S. Basil might mistake the occasion of that Oxe's teares.

Donne (Sermons)

34. I never read poetry. It might soften me.

General Hindenburg (1912)

35. 1. After vainly travelling abroad in hope of relief he died unmarried.

2. He died of erysipelas in the head, contracted by attending a political meeting.

3. He was always eccentric; and his behaviour one night at dinner was so strange that a guest intervened. He was placed under restraint at Norwood, in Surrey, and died without issue.

De Finibus Bonorum (from the D.N.B.*)*

36. Interviewing Americans – like talking with posterity from the other side of the Styx.

*Byron (*Ravenna Journal*)*

37. Forward, you lazy rascals, and fulfil the Prophecies!

Admiral Napier shouting to the troops at the Siege of Acre (1840)

38. The freedom of the rose-tree is the rose.

George Macdonald

39. Intellects becalmed in the smoke of Trafalgar.

A Quarterly *reviewer, of the Admiralty (1860)*

40. He that is full of himself goes out of company as wise as he came in.

Benjamin Whichcote

41. Never apologize for showing feeling. Remember that when you do so you apologize for *truth*.

Disraeli

42. A man should stand in a certain awe of his own prejudices, as of aged parents or monitors. They may in the end prove wiser than he.

Hazlitt

43. If I be not deceived, it is the distinctest teaching to put everything in his proper place.

Archbishop Abbot (on Jonah*)*

44. Cheat as little as you can.

Jowett (to a grocer who said it was impossible for an honest tradesman to live)

45. He that will do *all* that he can lawfully, would, if he durst, do something that is not lawful.

Jeremy Taylor

46. Going into the company of great men is to enter another world: a man should wait until the Call comes.

47. Stand on the Right – and let others pass you.

Directions on an Underground Escalator

48. People who count their chickens before they are hatched act very wisely; because chickens run about so absurdly afterwards that it is impossible to count them accurately.

Oscar Wilde (unpublished)

49. A strong case can scarce ever be stated too gently.

Bishop Hacket

50. He taught us to be critical, to be colourless, to be new.

Lord Acton, of Ranke

51. Christianity is good news: not good advice.

Dean Inge

52. This world and the next – and then *all* our troubles will be over.

General Gordon's aunt

1931

Do not take the first or the second that may present itself.
Sherlock Holmes, The Final Problem

1. We are born under a House of Lords like birds under a house of leaves: we live under a Monarchy as niggers live under a tropic sun.

G. K. Chesterton

2. We have the nonsense knocked out of us at a public school; and then we go to a university to have it all gently put back again.

Max Beerbohm

3. Above all, no enthusiasm.
   Archbishop Manners Sutton (Ordination Address, 1826)

4. Mes amis, croyez que je dors.
   An epitaph

5. Contact with the past and with the future, and a consistent purpose in life: that is success.
   Bertrand Russell

6. That rarest gift, the genius of reception.
   Disraeli

7. People complain that we have no literature nowadays. That is the fault of the Minister for Home Affairs.
   Napoleon

8. Veniet sicut fur.
   Motto in old Newgate Chapel

9. What has she done or suffered out of the common course of things? I love a little secret history.
   Dr. Johnson (of Miss Hudson, June 1783)

10. We owe this to Providence, and a series of happy accidents.
    Jowett (Sermon in Balliol Chapel, 1874)

11. Mon coeur, comme de la poussière, se soulevait derrière vos pas.
    Flaubert

12. Wash everything white – the easy, safe way.
    A laundry advertisement in the Daily Herald

13. Friends must be grafted in youth. Later friendships are only impressions, and stately as they may become, like elms, they have no tap-root.
    Thomas Gordon Hake

14. I dread nothing more than misplacing myself in my old age.
    Horace Walpole

15. A luxury, apt to degenerate into a nuisance.
> *Mr. Asquith (Budget Speech, 1907)*

16. (1) Rich, quiet, infamous people.
> *Macaulay*

   (2) The wonderless, the hard, the nice.
> *Osbert Sitwell*

17. The doctrine of Infallibility is a declaration of martial law.
> *Dean Inge*

18. Women who are either indisputably beautiful, or indisputably ugly, are best flattered upon the score of their understandings.
> *Lord Chesterfield*

19. The remark is just – but then you have not been under the wand of the magician.
> *Pitt, of Fox*

20. A man who could burst into tears at his own dinner-table on hearing a comparison made between St. Paul and St. John to the detriment of the latter, and beg that the subject might never be mentioned again in his presence, could never have been an *easy* companion.
> *A. C. Benson, of Dr. Arnold*

21. (a) The Three Rare Things (Sights of the Kingfisher)
     1. Clear memory of a Romantic Conversation.
     2. The meeting of Great Equals.
     3. Unremarked abbreviation of Pious Exercises.

   (b) The Three Wise Things (Perched Owls)
     1. To recognize the Ages of Man.
     2. To respect the Sleep of Friendship.
     3. To remember where your Shadow falls.

   (c) The Three Foolish Things (Spring Lambs)
     1. Deep sleep in an Unknown House.
     2. Setting to sea in a Borrowed Junk.
     3. Not to lag behind when the Elephant approaches a New Bridge.
> *Chinese Anthem, 1100 B.C.*

22. One hint I would give to all who attend or visit the sick. Come back and look at the patient *after* an hour's animated conversation with you.

Florence Nightingale

23. Men and women become good husbands and good wives from the necessity of remaining husbands and wives.

Lord Stowell (cited by Mr. Gladstone, 1879)

24. I should like to see a competition between these people and the Dutch.

A middle-aged Englishwoman at the Exhibition of Italian Painting (1929)

25. We shelled the Turks from 9 to 11: and then, it being Sunday, had Divine Service.

Commander, R.N., to Admiralty (1915)

26. Madam, the Wings of Opportunity are Fledged with the Feathers of Death.

Drake, to Elizabeth

27. That sort of thing is no use – unless you are well ribbed-up in trumps.

W. Dalton (on Auction Bridge)

28. The clergy are as like as peas: I cannot tell them apart.

Emerson

29. I have seen many bullies who were not cowards, but I never knew a coward who was not a bully.

Lord King, 1823

30. The whole range of his mind was from obscenity to politics, and from politics to obscenity.

Richard Savage, of Walpole

31. The best qualification of a Prophet is to have a good memory.

Lord Halifax

32. He liked what he considered to be the best conversation, including his own.

Times obituary notice

33. If two children upset a pot of jam, the disaster may be the fault, and the unapportionable fault, of both.

Lord Hewart, in a considered direction to a special jury on a question of Contributory Negligence

34. I see no reason to suppose that these machines will ever force themselves into general use.

Duke of Wellington on Steam Locomotives, 1827

35. There is a danger in being persuaded before one understands.

Bishop Wilson

36. Never sacrifice truth to simplicity, and remember it usually contradicts common sense.

Henry Ward

37. No wise man ever wished to be younger.

Swift

38. Enthusiasm for goodness shows that it is not the habit of the mind.

Coventry Patmore

39. What the Imagination seizes as Beauty must be Truth.

Keats

40. Consuetudo sine ratione, vetustas erroris est.

Hieronymus Pius, A.D. 590

41. If the fool would persist in his folly he would become wise.

Blake

42. A hamper is undoubtedly requisite under the present circumstances. It must contain several pots of superior jam.

Lord Curzon, aged 9, writing from school

43. Genius is the effort of the idea to assume a definite form.

Fichte

44. She's going about like an accident, looking for somewhere to happen.

From a serial story in the Sporting Times, *1911*

45. Society from top to bottom is permeated with a thousand aristocracies and a thousand democracies.

M. B. Douglas

46. He was as sure of himself at the head of the British army as a country gentleman on the soil which his ancestors had trod for generations, and to whose cultivation he had devoted his life.

Mr. Churchill, of Lord Haig

47. Il eut l'intention des grandes choses qu'il fit.

Michelet, of Richelieu

48. Bargain making, or the desire of having the credit for buying cheap, is very close to an infringement of the principle of honesty.

Richard Duppa

49. His memory was like a Scarf:
His common sense like a Buzzing of Bees:
His imagination like a Chime of Bells:
His thoughts like a Flight of Starlings:
His understanding like a Torn Breviary.

Rabelais

50. Something inherently mean in action! Even the creation of the Universe disturbs my idea of the Almighty's greatness.

Coleridge

51. Education enables you to express assent or dissent in graduated terms.

William Cory

52. So, then, as darkness had no beginning, neither will it ever have an end. The light doth but hollow a mine out of the infinite extension of the darkness. And ever upon the steps of the light treadeth the darkness; yea, springeth in fountains and wells amidst it, from the secret channels of its mighty sea.

George Macdonald, Phantastes

1932

1.   Who pays the piper?
         I, said John Bull.
         Whoever plays the fool,
         I pay the piper.
Popular song of 1832

2. Talk as much as possible to women. They ask so many questions.
Disraeli's advice to a young man

3. It is a good thing to speak the truth: but it is a better thing to know the truth and to talk about date-stones.
Arab proverb

4. What passes in the world for enterprise is often only a want of moral principle.
Hazlitt

5. At any rate, they keep out the half-witted.
Lord Bloomfield, of competitive examinations

6. It is a great presumption to send our passions upon God's errands.
William Penn

7. Nothing has an uglier look to us than Reason, when it is not of our side.
Lord Halifax

8. No patriot would ever say, 'My country, right or wrong.' It is like saying, 'My mother, drunk or sober.'
G. K. Chesterton

9. Americans go deeply into the surface of things.

Henry Ward

10. The right of a man to be buried in his own churchyard is acknowledged by our most authoritative writers: but I know of no rule of law which gives him the right to have a large trunk or chest buried in his company.

Lord Stowell (1834)

11. In language, the ignorant have prescribed laws to the learned.

Richard Duppa

12. We should have stood by, with folded hands, and what countenance we could command.

Mr. Asquith (September 1914)

13. Society of Contradictory Overseers.

Attempt by the Chinese Ambassador in 1881 to convey the sense of 'Protestant Episcopal Church'

14. The only way to deal with him is to be the last to leave his room.

Lord Lansdowne, of the Czar

15. * * * * * * * * * * * * * * * *

John Henry Newman

(What did he say? Oh, I don't know – but he *looked* at me.
An Oriel undergraduate)

16. I clearly foresee the day when this vainglorious and immoral people will have to be put down.

The Prince Consort, of the French (1860)

17. As natural as the box on the ear to a child.

German proverb

18. He uses figures as if they were adjectives.

A Treasury view of Lloyd George

19. Then, as a pianist runs his hand across the keyboard, from treble to bass, the bombardment began. The flashes lit up my tiny cabin like a flickering firelight.

Mr. Churchill

20. His face was one that nature had neither formed nor fondled nor finished, at all. Yet he carried this featureless disc as with the warranted assurance of a warning headlight, or a glaring motor lamp.

Henry James

21. The enthusiasm of the world cannot be roused by the commentary in small and subtle characters which alone can tell the whole truth.

George Eliot

22. Dear Sir

I apply for the position in your office and refer you to my principals Messrs. Eltzbacher, Cologne.

Yours sincerely
Ernest Cassel
Letter of Sir E.C. applying successfully for the post of confidential clerk to Mr. Bischoffsheim (1870)

23. It is only by a licence of speech, or by an enlargement at least of the signification of terms, that the name of charity can be given to a testamentary bequest, even though it be directed to benevolent uses.

Mr. Gladstone (1863)

24. We must be careful not to fix a passing impression of evil by demanding that it should be confessed.

Jowett

25. Never read by candlelight anything smaller than the Ace of Clubs.

Advice of Sir Henry Halford, President of the Royal College of Physicians, 1842

26. I described the Turkish attitude as incredible: Monsieur Bompard, with greater eloquence, denounced it as a crime.

Lord Curzon's Report to the Cabinet on the Lausanne Conference

27. All space is slightly curved.

Einstein

28. (1) The Three Good Things
    a. Certainty held in Reserve.
    b. Unexpected Praise from an Artist.
    c. Discovery of Nobility in Oneself.

   (2) The Three Bad Things
    a. Unworthiness crowned.
    b. Unconscious Infraction of the Laws of Behaviour.
    c. Friendly Condescension of the Imperfectly Educated.

   (3) The Three Things of both Good and Bad Effect
    a. Triumphant Anger.
    b. Banquets of the Rich.
    c. Honour preserved.
    Inscription found on a fragment of Wall of China (200 B.C.)

29. Speculation and conjecture as to the existence or non-existence of secret clauses in international treaties is a public privilege, the maintenance of which depends upon official reticence.
    Reply of Earl Percy to Mr. Weir in the House of Commons on the Anglo-French Agreement (11 August 1904)

30. What leapings of the heart must there not have been throughout that long warfare! What acts of devotion and desperate wonders of courage!

    H. G. Wells (of prehistoric man)

31. His mind gave way during the sittings of the Commission, and their proposals for a change of system were allowed to drop.
    De Morbis Excellentium Virorum (From the D.N.B.: Life of A. Panizzi)

32. Jaufre Rudel was a very noble man. He fell in love with the Countess of Tripoli, in spite of never having seen her, because of the good report of her he had from pilgrims from Antioch; and he made many poems about her with good tunes, but with words that were inferior.

Provençal Biography

33. Forces, Frauds, Inchoations, and Acts of Stellionate.

Lord Bacon's four divisions of crime

34. I don't know what you would call a regular life, but I mean by it a life in which one habitually breakfasts at eight.

Bishop Creighton (February 1871)

35. People sometimes talk as if in a future life they would have a sort of prescriptive *right* to our company. If so, the unseen world holds new terrors indeed.

A. C. Benson

36. Our military advisers, if they had their way, would garrison the moon in order to protect us from Mars.

Lord Salisbury (Debate on Strategic Points of the Empire)

37. The ardour which we do not share, chills us.

Coventry Patmore

38. The value of money has been settled by general consent to express our wants and our property, as letters were invented to express our ideas; and both these institutions, by giving more active energy to the powers and passions of human nature, have contributed to multiply the objects they were designed to represent.

Gibbon

39. Old Lord Burleigh has the appearance of a Pharisee just rebuffed by a gospel bon mot.

Keats, Letters

40. You do not need to hear a man say seven words to know him.
Five or six are enough.

*A Swiss peasant, 28 September 1787 (overheard by the
Revd. J. C. Lavater)*

41. Love is respectful and timorous.

Dr. Johnson

42. Its colour is the colour of the furthest apple-green and faint
golden edges of the sky at dawn; it is as cool as the air of an early
April morning; it is full of the scents of an upland with the dew
still on the wild flowers.

From a wine-merchant's catalogue: of a Rhine wine

43. He reads as other men breathe.

Lord Houghton, of Mr. Gladstone

44. Christ said, judge not at all. But we must judge.

Dean Inge

45. A discharge of crackers in the distance indicated that the local
methods of averting disaster were in progress.

Consular Report of a Solar Eclipse in the South Seas

46. Stop, Sir, stop – go away: I cannot bear your style.

Malherbe on his death-bed, to a priest

47. In all of us, the excited amateur has to die before the artist can
be born.

F. H. Bradley

48. It will scarcely be contended that our position as guarantor of
French credit is one of special privilege or advantage.

Mr. Balfour (1917)

49. Never come back to me with a *bargain*.

Wertheimer, to a young partner

50. Want of friends argues either want of humility or of courage, or
both.

Bishop Van Mildert

51. Strong brother in God and last companion, Wine.

Hilaire Belloc

52. **NO ROAD BEYOND THE CEMETERY**
Opinion of the Slough Borough Council, stated on a notice-board near Bourne End Church

1933

Combien de royaumes nous ignorent!

1. Oh, how hard it is to be shallow enough for a polite audience!

John Wesley

2. Dull people, not content with their advantage, wish to persuade us that we are all dull.

From a serial story in Belgravia *(1877)*

3. No great country was ever saved by good men, because good men will not go the length that may be necessary.

Horace Walpole

4. To speak highly of one with whom we are intimate is a form of egotism.

Hazlitt

5. Never say where you have been, or where you are going; and never ask for anything unless you are pretty sure to get it.

Lord Esher (1892)

6. Voyaging is victory.

Burton

7. Be careful with those who have few intimates.

F. H. Bradley

8. The true doctrine of Sovereignty is that of continuity: that is, that the sovereign power always resides somewhere, and that any attempt to restrict its exercise in any way at all is absolutely ineffective *ab initio*. That is a different thing from saying that the Sovereign cannot divide itself into several bodies in which, taken together, the totality of Sovereignty still resides.

Opinion of All the Judges of England in the Meekes case
(1864)

9. It is hard to come *down* the social ladder without tumbling off.

Samuel Butler

10. When three of us are together, there is certainly a master for me among them.

Confucius

11. If Cotes had lived – we might have known something.

Sir Isaac Newton

12. Actus legitimi conditionem non recipiunt neque diem.

Corpus Juris Canonici

13. When I hear a man talk of Sound Finance, I know him for an enemy of the people.

A Hyde Park orator, to an interrupter

14. Intemperance in talk makes a dreadful havoc in the heart.

Bishop Wilson

15. To do good work a man should no doubt be industrious. To do great work he must certainly be idle as well.

Henry Ward

16. Reflect, gentlemen, how many disputes you must have listened to, which were interminable because neither party understood either his opponent or himself.

Cardinal Newman (1858)

17. A crocus.
    Prison slang for Medical Officer (Dartmoor Report)

18. His face had that quality, common among the military in all communities, of looking like a profile even when seen from in front, so detached and inexpressive was it.
    H. G. Wells

19. The humanity of the United States can never reach the sublime.
    Keats, Letters

20. Don't go on with that, Mr. Asquith. The country isn't interested.
    The senior waiter, at a club dinner; with reference to the Land Tax

21. Restless, grasping, and quarrelsome, Europeans must be produced by the ocean.
    Peruvian superstition

22. (1) I saw Napoleon at Elba. He had a dusky grey eye – what would be called a vicious eye in a horse.
    (2) Lord John Townshend told me he had always foreseen the Coalition Ministry could not last, for he was at Court when Mr. Fox kissed hands, and he observed George III turn back his ears and eyes just like a horse at Astley's when the rider he has determined to throw is getting on him.
    Lord John Russell

23. Never laugh feebly at what you know to be wrong.
    Bishop Creighton

24. He was not a great churchman; and still less an ecclesiastical diplomat. He was a Secretary of State for Religion.
    A. C. Benson, of Archbishop Randall Davidson

25. People who do not observe, cannot converse.
    Balfour Browne, K.C.

26. And lastly let us salute the compulsive genius of British statesmen who confronted the sun in his march and rolled back the onset of night.

Mr. Churchill, of the Daylight-Saving Act

27. He had one eminently innocent passion. He was a devoted lover of flowers.

The Times *on Leopold II (1909)*

28. Regarded as a game, chess is more intellectual than life, or bridge.

Thomas Hardy

29. Roman Catholics claim to be infallible; Anglicans to be always right.

Steele

30. Women never dine alone. When they dine alone they don't dine.

Henry James, The Given Case

31. Logic is only rhetoric which has become irresistible by repetition.

Lord King (1826)

32. It was not the dust that repelled him, but the dustiness of the laurels.

Lord Crewe, of Lord Rosebery

33. English statesmen never see a question as part of a whole.

The Prince Consort

34. He could tolerate even the intolerant: it were a smaller feat than this to tolerate inferiority.

Gladstone of A. H. Hallam (unpublished)

35. They spend immeasurable periods of time in standing rather vaguely to attention; and seem to look on this one act as a substitute for all mental energy, and a discharge of all moral obligation.

Confidential report on the proficiency of warrant officers in the Army Service Corps (1903)

36. The Apostles' creed need not detain us long.

> *Bishop of Gloucester (opening of article on Christian*
> *Doctrine, April 1932)*

37. They act like generals before stategy was thought of.

> *A Treasury view of the Bank of England*

38. Lawyers are against legal reform.

> *Lord Loreburn*

39. It is very immoral and very unfair that any man should marry for money who does not want it.

> *Disraeli*

40. You can trust all Englishmen except those who talk French.

> *Bismarck*

41. There is no greater folly than to seek to correct the natural infirmities of those we love.

> *Fielding*

42. If you produce a larger amount of cultivated talent than there is a demand for, the surplus is very likely to turn sour.

> *Lord Stowell*

43. Romanists assert that Christ meant to found a universal theocratic empire. I deny it absolutely.

> *Dean Inge*

44. Never explain: never apologize: never repeat the mistake.

> *Jowett*

45. To be right in great and memorable moments is perhaps the thing we should most desire for ourselves.

> *George Eliot*

46. The Church was no more discredited by the War than the Ark was discredited by the Flood.

> *G. K. Chesterton*

47. Some people's education merely gives a fixed direction to their stupidity.

Lord Cromer

48. Suppose the Prime Minister and the Chancellor of the Exchequer were each to be asked what day the session would be over. Lord Palmerston would reply that it was the intention of Her Majesty to close the session on the 18th of August. Mr. Gladstone would possibly premise that inasmuch as it was for Her Majesty to decide upon the day which would be most acceptable to herself, it was scarcely compatible with Parliamentary etiquette to ask her ministers to anticipate such decision: but presuming that he quite understood the purport of the Right Honourable gentleman's question, of which he was not entirely assured, the completion of the duties of the House of Commons, and the formal termination of the sitting of the Legislature, being two distinct things, he would say that Her Majesty's ministers had represented to the Queen that the former would probably be accomplished about the 18th of August, and that such day would not be unfavourable for the latter, and, therefore, if the Sovereign should be pleased to ratify that view of the case, the day he had named would very likely prove to be that enquired after by the Right Honourable gentleman.

Quarterly Review (1855)

49. The sleep of friendship is its death.

Richard Duppa (1829)

50. "ΕΓΧΕΙ.

A motto

51. Who can hide magnanimity, stands on the supreme degree of human nature.

Revd. J. C. Lavater

52. Tout ce qui finit mérite le mépris.

Queen Christina of Sweden

TWELVE REFLECTIONS

1934

S'accorder, c'est déjà vieillir; ou bien s'extasier.

1. Never assume that habitual silence means ability in reserve.

2. The point of contact between education and frivolity is the need for talk.

3. What a vital difference between seriousness and solemnity!

4. Jews think of money as a sailor thinks of the sea.

5. The devil finds some mischief still for hands that have not learnt how to be idle.

6. The fine flower of stupidity blossoms in the attempt to appear less stupid.

7. Wit is a new and apt relation of ideas: humour, of images.

8. Good taste is good *sense*.

9. Young people should beware of falling in love with the opportunity of marrying.

10. The worst sin of the sensualist is to sentimentalize.

11. There is a social level at which intellect is superfluous; and an intellectual level at which rank is invisible.

12. The dust of exploded beliefs may make a fine sunset

LIVRE SANS NOM

[*This is the last* Livre sans Nom, *unprinted, date probably 1938 or early 1939. The last half of the reflections are anonymous, but by the same authors as the first half. The key is given at the end.*]

1. How deep is my decay! It is long since I saw the Duke of Chou in a dream.

Confucius

2. Never fight uneducated people except with their own weapons.
Lord Lyndhurst (overheard by Mr. Gladstone at dinner: November 1843)

3. Drink plenty of port, Sir! In a climate like ours you must drink port.

The Principal of Brasenose to Lord Haig as an under-graduate (1882)

4. The Psalmist wanted to sing something, but he never seems to have made up his mind clearly what he wanted to sing.

George Moore

5. Don't expect too much: and don't attempt too little.

Jowett

6. Slow givers give meanly, or with grandeur.

Revd. J. C. Lavater

7. The fresh, fair, ever so habitually assured, yet ever so easily awkward, Englishman.

Henry James

8. Nothing is more fatal to a school than obtrusive religion.
Revd. Edward Thring

9. La religion met à la portée de tous les vertus des grandes âmes.
Comtesse Diane

10. Too small a difference exists, at our Universities, between the sons of noblemen and the sons of commoners. The University, in term-time, is a foretaste of the world, where an immense difference exists.

Mr. Gladstone in conversation with Lady Rothschild:
February 1874

11. At every crisis he crumpled. In defeat, he fled; in revolution, he abdicated; in exile, he remarried.

Mr. Churchill, of the Kaiser

12. A man usually does his best work just before he is found out.

Dean Inge

13. Professors and rhetoricians invent systems and principles. Real statesmen are inspired by nothing else than an instinct for power, and a love of their country.

Disraeli, to Bülow

14. Tout nous dispute à Dieu.

Abbé Roux

15. Every man's censure is first moulded in his own nature.

George Herbert, Jacula Prudentum

16. Never be afraid to think yourself fit for anything for which your friends think you fit.

Dr. Johnson

17. Umbrellas are not allowed in the Vatican since the Pope's staff broke into blossom.

Oscar Wilde

18. Mastery often passes for egotism.

Goethe

19. Two thirds of the whole . . . is collected, without difficulty or friction, without any necessity for the taxpayer to draw a cheque or even open his purse, and almost without his being made aware that he is being taxed at all – I said, almost.

Mr. Asquith, on deduction of tax from dividends at
source: Budget Speech, 1908

20. The Parthian shot is the initiative of the weak: obstinacy, the strength of the sensitive.

Henry Ward

21. While philosophers were looking for a characteristic to distinguish man from other animals, inconsistency ought not to have been forgotten.

Richard Duppa

22. A sound creed, and a bad morality: that's the root of wisdom.

R. L. Stevenson

23. Few people would not be the worse for complete sincerity.

F. H. Bradley

24. You must either give people what they are used to, or what they don't understand.

George Eliot

25. It is constantly assumed that when the lion 'lies down with the lamb', the lion becomes lamb-like. But that is mere brutal annexation and imperialism on the part of the lamb. That is simply the lamb absorbing the lion, instead of the lion eating the lamb. The real question is, can the lion lie down with the lamb and still retain his royal ferocity? That is the problem the Church attempted: that is the miracle she achieved.

G. K. Chesterton

26. Should not the president of a dinner-table treat it like a battlefield, and let the guest that sinks descend?

George Meredith

*　　*　　*

27. It is a rare quality to know the best time and manner of yielding what it is impossible to keep.

28. I have always thought that every woman should marry, and no man.

29. The excitable; the venal; the worthless.

30. La question arrive souvent terriblement longtemps après la réponse.

31. Who loves, will not be adored.

32. La vraie séparation est celle qui ne fait pas souffrir.

33. I suppose everyone can do *something* better than other people: and he had better do it.

34. You can force anything on society, so long as it has no sequel.

35. Telle humilité provient d'orgueil: tel orgueil provient d'humilité.

36. Only one Italian author is mentioned in Erasmus.

37. A triangle in a hot-house.

Of modern novels

38. Perhaps the most lasting pleasure in life is the pleasure of *not* going to church.

39. When was the fatal coquetry inherent in superfluous authorship ever quite content with the ready praise of friends?

40. The deadliest foe to virtue would be complete self-knowledge.

41. A false ghost no more disproves the existence of ghosts than a forged banknote disproves the existence of the Bank of England.

42. An expert is one who knows so much about so little that he neither can be contradicted, nor is worth contradicting.

43. *If* you find yourself in a disorderly crowd, always remember, whatever happens, hold your umbrella *down*.

44. Brave as she was, and brave by intellect . . . .

45. Few tasks are more difficult than for a young woman under a cloud to hoodwink old women of the world.

46. There is a danger of mannerism even in simplicity.

47. Genius and stupidity never stray from their paths: talent wanders after every light.

48. It is important that young people should be bred up with affluent notions: even if there is a risk of luxury, it will be better luxury, and selfishness is none the worse for being a little less coarse.

49. Our friend felt a certain surprise, for the personage before him seemed to trouble a vision which was vague only when not confronted with the reality. As soon as the reality dawned, the mental image, retiring with a sigh, became substantial enough to suffer a slight wrong.

50. To learn from the near at hand may be called the key to love.

51. Nations on the gold standard are ships whose gangways are joined.

52. Tie it well, and let it go.

KEY

1 = 50	14 = 35	27 = 21	40 = 23
2 = 43	15 = 52	28 = 13	41 = 25
3 = 33	16 = 36	29 = 10	42 = 20
4 = 47	17 = 30	30 = 17	43 = 2
5 = 46	18 = 34	31 = 6	44 = 22
6 = 31	19 = 37	32 = 9	45 = 26
7 = 49	20 = 42	33 = 3	46 = 5
8 = 48	21 = 27	34 = 18	47 = 4
9 = 32	22 = 44	35 = 14	48 = 8
10 = 29	23 = 40	36 = 16	49 = 7
11 = 51	24 = 39	37 = 19	50 = 1
12 = 38	25 = 41	38 = 12	51 = 11
13 = 28	26 = 45	39 = 24	52 = 15